WHAT PEOPLE ARE SAYING ABOUT *LEGACY*

"*Legacy* is a challenge to every man to intentionally become the man God has called him to be. The examples from Scripture are shared in a clear and practical way that men can easily relate to through Jamie's personal and candid style of writing. I recommend this excellent book for personal reading as well as group study and discipleship."— **Dr. Stephen R. Tourville**, *PennDel Ministry Network Superintendent*

"In Rocky V, Rocky tells a young Tommy Gunn, 'I didn't hear no bell yet!' It's not too late. You can build a powerful legacy and Jamie's book shows you how. It's practical, easy to read, and introduces you to men from the Bible that serve as powerful role models and mentors. Whether you are reading this for your personal devotions or as part of a men's small group, you will find *Legacy* both challenging and inspiring!"— **Tom Rees**, *HonorBound Men's Director, PennDel Ministry Network*

"Jamie Holden does a masterful job of analyzing the lives of men in the Scriptures, looking at how each one left a legacy that addresses areas men face and can understand. He brings each story to life in a way men can follow in their own lives. Jamie develops this theme with personal illustrations and challenges men to live lives beyond themselves, with an eye to those who will follow them. This book is a testament to Jamie's own life of having overcome struggles that all men face. We can live a life worth following when we follow the examples God has given us in the Bible. Jamie draws out the legacies of biblical men of God, so that we might be men of God in our times."— **Bobby Basham**, *Potomac Men's Director, Executive Director of Royal Rangers*

"A man's life can change on a phrase. James Holden's book *Legacy* is loaded with thought-provoking truths that not only cause pause for reflection, but motivate to action. Because we men have a deep longing to make our lives count for more than a paycheck, *Legacy* wisely insists that we find meaning by living biblically. Each chapter highlights both well-known and lesser-known men of the Bible that left their mark on the times in which they lived. Holden challenges us men to make our mark on the times in which we live by leaving an intentional, godly *Legacy*. Whether for personal devotion or a men's study group, start your *Legacy* by applying this motivating and practical book."— **Brian C. Donnachie**, *NJ Assemblies of God Men's Ministry Director; Lead Pastor, Living Hope Worship Center; Conference Speaker*

"Jamie has a definite call on his life to assist men with their God-given responsibilities for manhood. His commitment to his called assignment is evident through his life and ministry. I appreciate Jamie's vision for this most needed mission in the body of Christ."—**Rick Allen**, *National LFTL Director, Assemblies of God*

"Knights are legends of examples of how to live life and, further, leave a legacy. Jamie Holden has identified a code of ethics for each of us to live by to develop our own legacy. Each man of God should seek to follow these examples and to live life accordingly."—**Dr. Darrel Billups**, *National Coalition of Ministries to Men, Executive Director*

"The next generation needs godly examples to follow. I appreciate leaders like Jamie Holden who encourage men to consider the legacy of their lives. My prayer is that the Lord will continue to raise up Spirit-empowered men in every home, workplace, church, and community."—**Tom Groot**, *Assemblies of God National Men's Ministry and Christian Education Director*

LEGACY

LIVING A LIFE THAT LASTS

JAMES J. HOLDEN

MORNING JOY MEDIA
Spring City, Pennsylvania

Published by Morning Joy Media. Visit www.morningjoymedia.com for more information on bulk discounts and special promotions, or e-mail your questions to info@morningjoymedia.com.

Design: Debbie Capeci
Author Photos (on cover and in back matter): Kristal Bentley

Cataloging-In-Publication Data

Subject Headings:

1. Christian life 2. Men's Issues 3. Spiritual formation.

ISBN 978-1-937107-52-9 (pbk)
ISBN 978-1-937107-53-6 (ebook)

Printed in the United States of America

I would like to dedicate this book to:

Roland Coon

Dan Courtney

Terry Drost

John Knudson

Ross Mullin

Paul Poole

Wayne Schaffer

I am forever grateful to each of these men. When God first gave me the vision to start the Mantour Conferences, these men embraced the vision and opened the doors of their churches to host the Mantours. Because of their willingness to take the plunge with me, we were able to get the Mantour Conferences off the ground. All the men who are reached and all the lives who are changed through the Holy Spirit working through the Mantours are part of these seven men's legacy! I dedicate this book to them.

CONTENTS

INTRODUCTION

Honor. Courage. Chivalry. Justice. Mercy. Generosity. Faith. Nobility. Hope. These are the traits legends are made of—they are the code of a knight!

The legends of knights, damsels in distress, and roundtables have stood the test of time. Women yearn for a knight in shining armor to save the day. Men admire their heroism and courage.

Knights were men who lived by a code of ethics. A knight believed his legacy was forged when he:

- Feared God and maintained God's church
- Served the liege lord (his employer) in valor and faith
- Protected the weak and defenseless
- Gave support to widows and orphans
- Refrained from the wanton giving of offense
- Lived by honor and for glory
- Despised financial reward
- Fought for the welfare of all
- Obeyed those placed in authority
- Guarded the honor of fellow knights
- Avoided unfairness, meanness, and deceit
- Kept the faith
- At all times spoke the truth

- Persevered to the end in any enterprise begun
- Respected the honor of women
- Never refused a challenge from an equal
- Never turned the back upon a foe.[1]

The world could sure use some modern-day knights! Men who are concerned about living a life that lasts. Men who care what their legacy will be.

I remember watching an episode of the TV show *Bonanza*. I grew up watching reruns of this classic Western centered around Ben Cartwright and his three sons, Adam, Hoss, and Little Joe.

I loved this show, especially when they would do a comical episode. One of my favorite episodes was named "A Knight to Remember." In this episode there was a man who was a banker for a living. He felt like his life had no meaning, like he wasn't making a difference, like he had no legacy. He didn't feel he was living a life that would last. So he decided to do something about it.

He grew up reading stories about King Arthur and the Knights of the Roundtable. These were men with legacies, men who were remembered throughout history. So the banker decided to go buy an old suit of armor and start policing the Wild West!

Of course, a man riding around in a suit of armor naturally sticks out like a sore thumb in the Old West. The man sees a stagecoach being held up, and rides in to save the day. Adam Cartwright was on the stagecoach, and ends up riding with the knight, trying to catch the robbers. You should watch the entire episode on YouTube. It is a great episode filled with lot of laughs as this old banker tries very ineptly to be a Knight of the Roundtable in a world where rifles and six-shooters rule the day.

What sticks out in this episode is that this man wanted to be remembered. He wanted to matter. He felt the drive to make a difference

---

1 The Song of Roland—Charlemagne's Code of Chivalry

in the world. This banker-turned-knight wanted a legacy that would stand the test of time. I think all men deal with this issue.

All men want one thing in life—to be remembered. We all want to have a legacy. Luckily for us, all people—from Adam, the first man ever created, to the next person to breathe their last breath—have a legacy. The issue we need to examine is, are we leaving behind a good legacy or a bad legacy? How will we be remembered?

I remember when my mom passed away, my sister and I had to find a tombstone for her grave. This job was extremely difficult for us, not just because of the grief we felt, but because we wanted her headstone to reflect who she was, her legacy, how we wanted her to be remembered. We struggled for days, trying to find something worthy of this amazing woman, and eventually we found just the right headstone and epitaph to describe her and her heart of devotion to God.

Guys, what would be written on your tombstone? What is your legacy?

Would it be "He was a man of God"?

Maybe, "A devoted husband and father."

For some it may not be so flattering.

"He was an angry, hateful man."

"He left."

"He was a cheater, liar, and swindler."

The good news for every one of us is that, as long as we are still alive and breathing, we can continue to write our legacy. We can work to leave a legacy that honors God and encourages those we leave behind. We can live a life that lasts!

God can help you to create a legacy that future generations can look at and say, "Now there was a real man, a godly man!"

Throughout this book, I want to look through God's legacy book, the Bible, and show you portraits of different men who were truly godly men. I believe if we do what the people in the Bible did, then we will experience what they experienced. Through their example, we will learn how to become real men, godly men, men living a life that lasts.

You may ask, "Why do you think *you're* qualified to teach me about becoming a godly man?" My response is *I am not qualified*. I am not any better than any man who will read this book. I wrestle with the same struggles, issues, and demons that all men fight. I have no special qualification at all. However, the Christ who lives in me does. What I am about to share with you are the things the Holy Spirit used to help me through one of the darkest times in my life as I realized I needed to start rewriting my legacy. I, in turn, want to share these things with you in hopes that you will grow in spiritual maturity and become the man God created you to be. Let me briefly share my story with you.

I grew up in what I thought was a Christian home, with a saved father and mother. I went to Christian school my whole life. We attended the premier church in our area. We appeared to be the "perfect Christian family." It looked good to all around. However, it wasn't that way at all.

I felt called by God to the ministry, so when I graduated from high school I enrolled in Bible college. I was a relative success through my first two years. I was being mentored by a godly professor, and was handpicked my freshman year to lead men's groups on campus—I thought for sure I was the next Billy Graham. But things began to fall apart.

The godly, perfect father I thought I had began to get violent and angry. Things in our home began to deteriorate. From being around the godly professors at college, I had been seeing for a while that the "godly" father I grew up with was a farce. Of course, while growing up, there had been physical, mental, and emotional abuse, but we were told it was our fault and my mom's fault and we deserved it. Now, seeing other men of God and the way they acted, my dad didn't line up.

During my junior year of college it came out that my dad was leading a double life. My family was devastated. We didn't know what to do. Nothing we knew about him or his past was true. He was never a real Christian—he just put on a good show.

This was the man I had looked up to my whole life. I thought he was the model of a godly man and patterned myself after him. I wanted to be just like him! Now to find all this out devastated me. I came to realize I had no idea what a godly man was. My thinking on this subject was totally twisted. The patterns and mindset I had developed turned out to actually be the ways of an abusive, deceptive man, not a godly one. I was recreating a bad legacy, and I had to make changes. I had to start over and relearn everything. I had to work through all my ideas of what a godly man was and examine them against the Bible. I had to repent and discard all the ungodly ways and replace them with new, biblical patterns.

I read many books on manhood, marriage, and parenting by godly pastors. I did Bible studies on the subject. But most importantly, I opened myself up to the Holy Spirit to shine his light on any areas that needed to change. He is always showing me things that need to be dealt with for me to be the man God wants me to become. It is a journey that I am deeply committed to for the rest of my life.

It took a lot of counseling and a long time to work through this stuff, but I finally worked through the hurt and pain. Since my mother's death, my dad has started attending church again, and I pray he gets serious about his walk with God as I try to daily show him God's love and forgiveness.

Then God began showing me the *why* of it all.

I began to see that the life and problems I have experienced are shared by millions of men around the world. So many men have grown up with a poor example for a legacy, and even more have grown up without any father in their lives. The only legacy these men know is *men don't stay.*

These men have the same problem I did. They have no idea what it means to be a real man of God.

Other men had good examples in their lives, but because of sinful choices they made, they find themselves staring at their legacy and thinking, "What happened? How did I make such a mess? How do I start over?"

Still others are honestly doing the best they can, but feel they can do better. This book is for these men too. All men can benefit from this book, not because I have all the answers, but because we all have the same question—*How will I be remembered?*

> **ALL MEN CAN BENEFIT FROM THIS BOOK, NOT BECAUSE I HAVE ALL THE ANSWERS, BUT BECAUSE WE ALL HAVE THE SAME QUESTION— HOW WILL I BE REMEMBERED?**

I feel it is my calling to share what I have learned, and to help men out of their situation so they can become all God wants them to be and can start recreating a new legacy, a godly legacy.

In this book, I would like to introduce you to some of the truly godly men that we see in the Bible and, through their examples, see how you can become all God wants you to be. We will look at the legacies they left behind for us to follow. It will change your life, your thinking, your actions, your family, your relationships, and, most importantly, your relationship with God.

My goal is to expose you to a variety of men, but I especially want to deal with some of the lesser-known men of the Bible who lived a life dedicated to godliness but have not been recognized as they should be. I want to shine a light on their legacies, and show you how you can follow their example. I am also going to focus on some of the better-known men who I have personally come to love through my studies. While all of these men have many different character qualities of a godly man, my purpose is to hone in on one main character trait that each particular man exhibited, the thing that is their shining legacy throughout the ages.

At the end of each chapter, there will be a Legacy Challenge geared to helping you develop the specific character trait that was examined. There will also be Extreme Legacy Challenges. These assignments are geared to the man who has a deep desire to become the man God wants him to be and will take whatever steps necessary for this to happen. They are deeper, more time-consuming challenges; however, I guarantee that the end result will make it worth it.

Finally, each chapter will end with a set of group study questions. I love the concept of men getting together and working through a book as a group, and these questions are geared to help start a discussion of the character traits in that chapter. I hope you use these questions in a group setting or at least work through them at home on your own. These questions will also be listed in the back of the book in our workbook section so you don't have to constantly flip back and forth to the chapter.

The workbook also has some questions designed for self-examination, and they include plenty of space for you to write in your answers. Finally, the workbook has a Legacy Thought to Remember for each chapter, which is one key thought to meditate on and/or memorize.

Guys, we have stated the mission. The goals are set. Join with me now as we begin an exciting adventure whose chief goal is to help us redefine our legacies as we endeavor to live lives that last!

1

THE MANASSEH LEGACY

REALIZING THE NEED
TO START OVER

As I began to prep and outline this book, I struggled as to which man's legacy to discuss first. The Bible is jam-packed with men who have amazing legacies for us to study. As I thought about it, I decided to start with a man that, in all of my reading and studying, I have never seen addressed in a chapter of a book, not to mention the very first chapter. Why?

Because for most of this man's life and history, his legacy left much to be desired. He wasn't known as a great man of faith, or a man who was even concerned about God or God's ways. Who is this man? King Manasseh.

When you compile the list of the most-known things about Manasseh, you wouldn't think anyone would hold him up as an example of developing a new legacy. However, he is the perfect man to start. He gives hope to every man who wants to leave his old life behind and start over with God.

Manasseh's life was a downward spiral of sin and evil. His legacy left a stench in the nostrils of anyone who came in contact with him. However, Manasseh shows every one of us that, no matter where we came from or how big of a mess we have made of our lives, it is never too late to start over and develop a new legacy of godliness!

We first read about Manasseh in 2 Kings 21. Manasseh became the king of Judah after the death of his father, Hezekiah.

Hezekiah was a great, godly king who loved God and served him faithfully. He was one of the few guys with a good eulogy in the book of 2 Kings. However, when it came to his son Manasseh, the apple not only fell far from the tree, but it rolled down the hill, over the cliff, into the river, and washed ashore many miles away.

They were nothing alike! Manasseh was a horrible king! His life's decisions not only devastated him, but millions of people around him. His actions as king make him one of the cruelest leaders in history. Let's look at a few highlights of his reign of terror and ungodliness:

1. He served the false gods of the Canaanites, which was completely forbidden for God's people.

2. He rebuilt the high places of worship to false gods that had previously been removed during times of revival.

3. He built altars to Baal and Ashtoreth, the two vilest gods of Canaan.

4. He bowed to the stars and worshipped them.

5. He participated in witchcraft, sorcery, and demon worship—the modern equivalent of a Satanist.

6. He set up burnt offerings and altars to other gods *inside* the temple of God, a HUGE no-no!

7. He murdered and burned his own son on an altar as a sacrifice to false gods.

8. He led God's people into satanic worship and serving false gods.

9. He murdered any Jew who refused to serve false gods. He killed so many of them that the Bible says the innocent blood of the martyrs he killed filled the streets of Jerusalem from end to end.

10. Tradition says he murdered the prophet Isaiah by sawing him in two as he hid in a hollow log (Hebrews 11:37).

11. He set up an Asherah pole in the temple of God. The worship of Ashtoreth involved male and female prostitution, so he basically turned the house of God into a brothel.

Manasseh was the most wicked king in Jewish history. How's that for a legacy!

Not exactly who you would think would be the first man in a book designed to help us develop a godly legacy! His reign of terror put fear into millions. It also captured the attention of God.

> *The LORD said through his servants the prophets: "Manasseh king of Judah has committed these detestable sins. He has done more evil than the Amorites who preceded him and has led Judah into sin with his idols. Therefore this is what the LORD, the God of Israel, says: I am going to bring such disaster on Jerusalem and Judah that the ears of everyone who hears of it will tingle. …I will wipe out Jerusalem as one wipes a dish, wiping it and turning it upside down. I will forsake the remnant of my inheritance and give them into the hands of enemies. They will be looted and plundered by all their enemies; they have done evil in my eyes and have aroused my anger from the day their ancestors came out of Egypt until this day" (2 Kings 21:10–15).*

God, in his holiness, had enough of Manasseh and his sin. As a result, he sent enemies against Manasseh. We see this in 2 Chronicles 33:11:

So the LORD brought against them the army commanders of the king of Assyria, who took Manasseh prisoner, put a hook in his nose, bound him with bronze shackles and took him to Babylon.

Ouch! You read that correctly—he was literally dragged off to Babylon via a chain hooked to his nose! Manasseh's reign of terror was put to an end under the mighty hand of God. Manasseh was bound and dragged off to Babylon.

However, God didn't abandon Manasseh. Even though Manasseh had committed such vile sins against God, God gave him a chance to repent and get his life straightened out.

Manasseh took God's gracious offer.

In his distress he sought the favor of the LORD his God and humbled himself greatly before the God of his ancestors. And when he prayed to him, the LORD was moved by his entreaty and listened to his plea; so he brought him back to Jerusalem and to his kingdom. Then Manasseh knew that the LORD is God.

NO MAN IS TOO FAR GONE TO START OVER AND CREATE A NEW LEGACY! THERE IS HOPE!

That is why we want to start off with Manasseh. I seriously doubt anyone reading this book has as horrible of a legacy as Manasseh. Maybe you do. Either way, this chapter is meant to show you that **no man is too far gone to start over and create a new legacy.** There is hope! We see it in this passage.

Manasseh, the most wicked dude in the entire Bible, started over. How did he do it? Let's look at the passage again.

In his distress he sought the favor of the LORD his God and humbled himself greatly before the God of his ancestors.

HE ADMITTED HE MADE A MESS OF HIS LIFE

Being dragged over 500 miles by a ring in your nose has a way of breaking a man! All of Manasseh's pride, arrogance, and self-sufficiency ended somewhere around the first time the dusty road made him sneeze. (Okay, the Bible doesn't say that, but you know somewhere on the trip he sneezed and it had to hurt really bad!) He realized all the pain not only *he* endured, but that the *entire kingdom of Judah* experienced, was because of his sin and rebellion.

Manasseh realized he brought all of this on himself, his chickens came home to roost, and he had to do something about it. That brings us to action number two.

HE HUMBLY REPENTED

Manasseh knew he had sinned. He knew he needed God's forgiveness. So he humbled himself and asked God to forgive him.

Now I don't believe this was a prisoner's conversion, hoping to get out on good behavior. He knew the Babylonians were ruthless men—when they took you, you didn't come back. A good outcome would be torture followed by life in a dungeon.

I believe Manasseh's repentance was genuine. A broken and destroyed Manasseh finally came to his senses and turned to God for forgiveness. He came to the end of himself, looked around at his legacy, and realized he had a lot to repent of in life. He truly committed himself to following and serving God. As a result, God restored Manasseh as king.

> And when he prayed to him, the LORD was moved by his entreaty and listened to his plea; so he brought him back to Jerusalem and to his kingdom. Then Manasseh knew that the LORD is God.

LEGACY: LIVING A LIFE THAT LASTS

God saw Manasseh's true repentance and he restored him. Once he was king again, Manasseh immediately began undoing the years of damage he had done.

MANASSEH'S REPENTANCE WAS FOLLOWED BY HEARTFELT CHANGE

Afterward he rebuilt the outer wall of the City of David, west of the Gihon spring in the valley, as far as the entrance of the Fish Gate and encircling the hill of Ophel; he also made it much higher. He stationed military commanders in all the fortified cities in Judah. He got rid of the foreign gods and removed the image from the temple of the LORD, as well as all the altars he had built on the temple hill and in Jerusalem; and he threw them out of the city. Then he restored the altar of the LORD and sacrificed fellowship offerings and thank offerings on it, and told Judah to serve the LORD, the God of Israel. …Manasseh rested with his ancestors and was buried in his palace. And Amon his son succeeded him as king.

Manasseh dedicated the rest of his life to serving God and rebuilding the nation he had earlier destroyed. It wasn't easy. He had to return and face the people he had ruled over so cruelly. He had to destroy all the idols and sinful high places in his nation. Repentance wasn't enough, action was needed.

Understand this: I don't believe in penitence at all; salvation is by grace, not works. But I do think there is something to be said for taking actions to fix the damage we have done.

Repentance requires a change in direction, and that includes no longer doing the sinful things we did before. We need to destroy them and start over. Manasseh shows us that if we want to develop a new legacy, we need to deal some deathblows to our old legacy. Then you have to work toward developing a new godly legacy by following God's commands. Manasseh destroyed his sinful ways, and then started worshipping God in the way God expected of his people.

As we bring this chapter to a close, I want to give a word of warning and a word of encouragement to you. Let's start with the warning.

God's will is for all men to abandon the sinful legacy we develop apart from him, and he will reward us accordingly. However, sometimes we still suffer the consequences of our former life.

What do I mean? Let's look a little further into Manasseh's legacy.

The warning comes because the story of Manasseh probably left you thinking, "Wow! What a great story of conversion and repentance to God. Manasseh started a new legacy and all went well from there forward."

Unfortunately, this is only partly true. There were consequences to Manasseh's years of sin. Allow me to explain. Manasseh's son, Amon, replaced him as king.

> **REPENTANCE REQUIRES A CHANGE IN DIRECTION, AND THAT INCLUDES NO LONGER DOING THE SINFUL THINGS WE DID BEFORE. WE NEED TO DESTROY THEM AND START OVER.**

Amon was twenty-two years old when he became king, and he reigned in Jerusalem two years. He did evil in the eyes of the LORD, as his father Manasseh had done. Amon worshiped and offered sacrifices to all the idols Manasseh had made. But unlike his father Manasseh, he did not humble himself before the LORD; Amon increased his guilt. Amon's officials conspired against him and assassinated him in his palace. Then the people of the land killed all who had plotted against King Amon, and they made Josiah his son king in his place.

Wait! Manasseh repented and started a new generation of godliness! How did this happen?!

Guys, sometimes we have to suffer the consequences of our actions. If a prisoner repents and changes, he still has to finish his sentence. Amon grew up for twenty years under the reign of terror of the unsaved Manasseh. He saw the way his father lived. He knew the murderous, idolatrous Manasseh. He saw his dad murder his own brother in a sacrifice. He saw years of sin and evil demonstrated before him, and he didn't choose to overcome it. As a result, his kingship was a disaster and he died in his sins.

Actions have consequences. That's why I wanted to issue the warning. We can always find love, acceptance, and forgiveness from God. He will always bless our desire to start a new legacy. However, life may not turn to gumdrops and daisies. Tough times and painful circumstances may result from previous decisions.

I know what you're thinking. "Way to bring the mood down, Jamie. I was pumped up after reading Manasseh's story. Now you tell me nothing will change."

That is not at all what I am saying. That's why I saved the encouragement for after the warning. Amon saw his father's sinful legacy, and he saw his father's reborn legacy. He made a choice to follow the sinful legacy. However, Manasseh's reborn legacy did bear fruit and prosper. What do I mean?

Well, the Bible tells us Amon was succeeded by his son, Josiah. Josiah became king at the age of eight. Josiah never knew his grandfather Manasseh as the evil dictator. He knew him as Grandpa Manasseh, a man who served God. He probably sat on his grandfather's knee as a child and heard him talk about the importance of loving and serving God. To Josiah, Grandpa Manasseh was a neat old guy who slipped him peppermint matzo candy and followed God wholeheartedly. He learned from his grandpa.

Manasseh's legacy of godliness is seen in the life of Josiah.

Josiah was eight years old when he became king, and he reigned in Jerusalem thirty-one years. He did what was right in the eyes of the LORD and walked in the ways of his father David, not turning aside to the right or to the left.

Josiah was a man of God who reformed the nation of Israel. As Grandpa Manasseh had done, Josiah went through his kingdom and removed all the idols and sin which his own father had restored during his two-year reign.

In the eighth year of his reign, while he was still young, he began to seek the God of his father David. In his twelfth year he began to purge Judah and Jerusalem of high places, Asherah poles and idols. Under his direction the altars of the Baals were torn down; he cut to pieces the incense altars that were above them, and smashed the Asherah poles and the idols. These he broke to pieces and scattered over the graves of those who had sacrificed to them. He burned the bones of the priests on their altars, and so he purged Judah and Jerusalem. In the towns of Manasseh, Ephraim and Simeon, as far as Naphtali, and in the ruins around them, he tore down the altars and the Asherah poles and crushed the idols to powder and cut to pieces all the incense altars throughout Israel. Then he went back to Jerusalem. In the eighteenth year of Josiah's reign, to purify the land and the temple, he sent Shaphan son of Azaliah and Maaseiah the ruler of the city, with Joah son of Joahaz, the recorder, to repair the temple of the LORD his God.

Josiah completely removed all the sin in Judah. He destroyed every idol and high place that his father had reinstalled after Manasseh destroyed them. He restored the temple of God to its previous glory. Josiah wholeheartedly served God and inspired the people of Judah to do the same.

Josiah removed all the detestable idols from all the territory belonging to the Israelites, and he had all who were present in Israel serve the LORD their God. As long as he lived, they did not fail to follow the LORD, the God of their ancestors. …So at that time the entire service of the LORD was carried out for the celebration of the Passover and the offering of burnt offerings on the altar of the LORD, as King Josiah had ordered. The Israelites who were present celebrated the Passover at that time and observed the Feast of Unleavened Bread for seven days. The Passover had not been observed like this in Israel since the days of the prophet Samuel; and none of the kings of Israel had ever celebrated such a Passover as did Josiah, with the priests, the Levites and all Judah and Israel who were there with the people of Jerusalem. This Passover was celebrated in the eighteenth year of Josiah's reign.

IT IS NEVER TOO LATE TO START A NEW, REBORN LEGACY!!

Manasseh's choice to repent, leave his sin, and follow God wholeheartedly resulted in his grandson, Josiah, leading the greatest revival in Jewish history. His legacy of leaving behind sin and following God wholeheartedly lived on through his grandson, Josiah.

Deuteronomy 5:9–10 says:

You shall not bow down to them or worship them; for I, the LORD your God, am a jealous God, punishing the children for the sin of the parents to the third and fourth generation of those who hate me, but showing love to a thousand generations of those who love me and keep my commandments.

This is a promise we can all hold on to as we pursue a new life of holiness and devotion to God. **It is never too late to start a new legacy!**

We have God's word that, when we live up to our end by repenting, turning from our old sinful ways, serving him wholeheartedly, and teaching our family to do the same, he will bless and show his love to our descendants.

Manasseh's life demonstrates this to us. His wicked life of sin and murder carried on for one generation in his son. His sin did have consequences. However, when he repented and turned to God, his legacy of righteousness carried on through the life of Josiah and resulted in a revival sweeping though the entire nation.

Guys, you too can start a new legacy. As Rocky Balboa said to Tommy Gunn in Rocky V, "I didn't hear no bell yet!"

It's not over! We haven't lost. It doesn't matter about your past or the shambles your life is in now. You can develop the Reborn Legacy! All God requires is for us to repent, turn from our wicked ways, and dedicate ourselves to wholeheartedly serve him and follow his commandments.

Manasseh was a man who made a remarkable reformation in his life. He repented of his sinful ways, turned to God for forgiveness, and followed him wholeheartedly. He completely transformed his life. God rewarded Manasseh's change through Josiah and his legacy.

This opportunity is there for every one of us. The Reborn Legacy teaches us that it's never too late to start a godly legacy if we make the choice to start developing godly character traits in our lives.

The rest of this book is geared toward showing you legacies and godly character traits we can all aspire to in our lives, legacies that will carry on for generations to come. Guys, we all will be remembered; the question is, *how* will we be remembered? There is still time to rewrite the answer to this question. We need to begin today.

In my life, I had to come to a point where I realized it was my job to start a new legacy (I hope you didn't skip the Introduction; if so, take time and read it). I had to stop blaming my dad for my problems and start accepting that the legacy I was leaving was my choice. I held the power to continue creating a bad legacy, and I held the power to repent and start a new legacy. It was a decision I had to make, and you need to make the same decision.

How will you be remembered? The choice is yours today!

Dear heavenly Father, Thank you for showing us both the good side and the bad side of Manasseh's life. Thank you for his inspirational story which gives me hope that, no matter what my legacy or what I have done in my life, I can start over today developing a new, godly legacy.

From this day forward, I am dedicating my life to serving you completely. Please forgive me for the times I have walked away or lived a life that isn't pleasing to you. From this moment forward, I choose to start working on my heart and life so that I can leave a legacy of which future generations can be proud. In Jesus' name, amen.

LEGACY CHALLENGES

Spend time alone with God, and allow the Holy Spirit to show you how you would be remembered if you died today. This may be hard to see the truth about yourself, but realizing which areas need to change is step one to starting a new legacy.

EXTREME LEGACY CHALLENGES

This chapter discusses the steps Manasseh took to literally destroy his old legacy. Identify some steps you can take to destroy your sinful legacy.

- What changes need to be made?
- What must you stop doing?
- What must you start doing?

Ask these questions of a spouse or close, trusted friend or mentor and get his or her advice. Then start the process of beginning a new legacy.

GROUP STUDY QUESTIONS

1. Manasseh had developed a horrible legacy, yet was able to change. What areas of your life do you need to repent of and change to begin starting a new legacy?

2. We discussed Manasseh's breaking point where he realized he needed to humble himself. What was your breaking point?

3. Why is it important to take actions to dismantle our old legacy in order to start a new one? What does this involve for you?

4. What did the warning toward the end of the chapter mean to you?

5. Did you ever stop and think about the fact that the way you live your Christian life in front of your children could affect their eternal souls?

6. How would you feel if you knew your children went to hell because of the poor example you set before them of Christianity?

7. What can you do to ensure this doesn't happen?

8. If you are single, what changes do you need to make to your spiritual life before God blesses you with a wife and kids?

9. Read Deuteronomy 5:9–10. What does this passage say to you as you start the journey toward a Reborn Legacy?

2

THE JONATHAN LEGACY

THE SECOND VERSE
NOT THE SAME AS THE FIRST

Gadgets. I love them. When I see those new gizmos advertized on TV, something inside of me stirs. Whether it's knives that cut through bricks, electric scissors, or some new miracle spot remover, I always let out a little grunt.

I love to go to stores and to the electronics department. I enjoy wandering through Staples and looking at all that the world of technology has to offer. Whenever I have free time while my sister does a women's ministry event, I head to Best Buy and just wander around, looking at all the new toys out there. I rarely buy, but I enjoy the show!

I remember the first time I bought a new printer. It was one of those all-in-one jobs that prints and scans. I never had a scanner before, so I set out to scan anything and everything. I took our family albums and scanned them onto a CD. Now every picture my family ever took is secure on disc.

As I went through the albums, I noticed a lot of pictures of me and my dad. I was always following him around idolizing him. If he had a rake, I had a toy rake. If he had a wheelbarrow, so did I. I always wanted to be near him. I looked up to him. I thought he could do no wrong. He was my dad and I wanted to be just like him.

Most young children are this way. They want to be with their daddy. Any amount of attention he gives them is like a pot of gold. As I grew older, I saw that the man I had looked up to and modeled myself after was not the man I thought. More than that, he was not the man I wanted to be.

Unfortunately, God began to show me just how much of a chip off the old block I was. I had seen my dad's actions and decisions leave my entire family ravished and devastated. Then I saw how I had become an abusive man who had no respect for women. I was rebellious. I was a deceitful man. I got trapped in pornography. I was irresponsible and immature, especially in financial matters. When I looked in the mirror, I didn't like what I saw!

NO MAN IS EVER DOOMED TO REPEAT HIS FATHER'S MISTAKES!

Realizing all this made me want change. Even though I called myself a Christian and was studying to go into ministry, I was not living the life of a godly man. I had to learn to think, act, talk, and live in a whole new way. I needed a different legacy, a new path founded on God's ways and principles.

I don't know where you are coming from. Maybe you had a great father, a godly father—I'm thrilled if you had this blessing. Maybe you grew up without a father and you have no idea how a godly man acts. Maybe you, like me, didn't have a godly example of a father and you desire to live totally different. Whatever your circumstances, you don't have to become a man you don't want to be. God can change you.

He can teach you how to live, act, and make better choices than your father made.

No man is ever doomed to repeat his father's mistakes! The second verse doesn't have to be the same as the first.

You can become a new man. You can create a different legacy. You can choose a different way. I did and so did the next man we are going to study. His name is Jonathan.

Jonathan saw the kind of man his father was and decided he didn't want to be that way. In the end, we will see that he became a man with a totally different heart than his father. We see this in the three main areas all men deal with: his relationship to God, his family life, and his work. Let's get started.

JONATHAN HAD A HEART FOR GOD, WHILE SAUL DIDN'T

The first area we look at is the different relationships Saul and Jonathan had with God. Throughout the book of 1 Samuel, we see that Saul had a surface relationship with God. He served God in a very selfish way. He only wanted God when he needed something. He basically wanted God to serve him.

Saul didn't feel the need to live according to God's standards and ways. We see this is in 1 Samuel 13 when Saul erected an altar and made a sacrifice to God. This was a blasphemous act by Saul. Samuel was supposed to make sacrifices, not Saul.

Saul lived a life of disobedience to God. He felt that it was all right for him to live the way he wanted to live. He saw no need to follow God's instructions. This is illustrated in 1 Samuel 15 as Saul was to lead an attack against the Amalekites. Let's look at God's instructions:

Now go, attack the Amalekites and totally destroy all that belongs to them. Do not spare them; put to death men and women, children and infants, cattle and sheep, camels and donkeys.

These instructions are pretty clear. Saul was to kill all of them, no highway option! However, the passage tells us how Saul handled it.

He took Agag king of the Amalekites alive, and all his people he totally destroyed with the sword. But Saul and the army spared Agag and the best of the sheep and cattle, the fat calves and lambs— everything that was good. These they were unwilling to destroy completely, but everything that was despised and weak they totally destroyed.

Saul disobeyed God by not destroying everything. As a result, God told Samuel that he was done with Saul. Saul's kingdom would be taken away from him and another man would take his place.

Later in 1 Samuel, we read that the new king would be David. It is when David enters the story that we see the difference between the spiritual lives of Saul and Jonathan.

Instead of going along with God's will and accepting that his kingdom would be given to David, Saul set out on a crusade to kill David. Forced to flee for his life, David made an escape to the desert region. It's here we can see that Jonathan had a different heart than Saul. He had a heart committed to God and God's will.

Jonathan had formed a deep friendship with David. He found in David a kindred spirit, dedicated to serving God. When David realized Saul wanted to kill him, he approached Jonathan for help. Jonathan agreed to find out if Saul really intended to kill David. If it was true, he agreed to help David escape.

But if my father intends to harm you, may the LORD deal with Jonathan, be it ever so severely, if I do not let you know and send you away in peace. May the LORD be with you as he has been with my father. But show me unfailing kindness like the LORD's kindness as long as I live, so that I may not be killed, and do not ever cut off your kindness from my family—not even when the LORD has cut off every one of David's enemies from the face of the earth (1 Samuel 20:13–15).

Jonathan knew it was God's will for David to replace Saul as king. You have to realize that, in normal circumstances, Jonathan would be in line to inherit his father's throne. However, he knew God's will was for David to become king.

Jonathan's heart and life were so in tune with God that he went along with the new plan and supported David. He didn't stab David in the back or seek a way to hold on to his position. Instead, he supported David and made a covenant with him.

Here's an interesting fact about these two men. I always thought that Jonathan and David were the same age. However, after studying this passage, I learned that Jonathan was at least ten years older than David. He was more of a mentor to David, giving him brotherly advice.

This is an important point to demonstrate how dedicated Jonathan was to submitting to God's will. He was willing to train and mentor the man who was going to take his place as the king. Anything David knew about leading an army or being a king, he learned from Jonathan. How did Jonathan bring himself to do this? Because he was totally committed to submitting to God's will.

Jonathan's heart was completely different than Saul's. He loved God and served God even when it cost him. Saul only served God when he wanted something from him. Jonathan obeyed God no matter what he asked.

I want this to encourage you. No matter what kind of spiritual life your father has, you can develop a strong, mature relationship with God. Even if your father is an atheist, you can have an unbelievable walk with God. You can develop a heart that is completely different from your father's. Jonathan did, and so can you.

JONATHAN WAS A FAMILY MAN, SAUL WASN'T

The second area that reveals the different heart Jonathan possessed is in relation to his family. Saul set a horrible example of a family man for Jonathan. Saul never put his family first. Quite the contrary. Saul always put himself first and used his family as pawns to suit his purposes. Let's return to 1 Samuel to see what I mean.

Saul was obsessed with killing David. He had no qualms in using his family to do it. Numerous times in the book of 1 Samuel we read of Saul using his children to trap David.

Saul said to David, "Here is my older daughter Merab. I will give her to you in marriage; only serve me bravely and fight the battles of the LORD." For Saul said to himself, "I will not raise a hand against him. Let the Philistines do that!" (1 Samuel 18:17).

Basically, Saul is selling his daughter to David. He used her to trap David into a fight with the Philistines in hopes that they would kill David. He had no love or respect for his daughter. He was just using her. This isn't the only time we see Saul do this.

> **YOU CAN DEVELOP A HEART THAT IS COMPLETELY DIFFERENT FROM YOUR FATHER'S.**

The story continues to tell us that after the Philistines fail to kill David, Saul backed out of the deal and gave his daughter to another man. However, he is still intent on killing David. Not being a very creative guy, Saul tries the same tactic again.

Now Saul's daughter Michal was in love with David, and when they told Saul about it, he was pleased. "I will give her to him," he thought, "so that she may be a snare to him and so that the hand of the Philistines may be against him." So Saul said to David, "Now you have a second opportunity to become my son-in-law" (1 Samuel 18:20–21).

Talk about second verse same as the first! Once again Saul uses his daughter to try and trap David in battle, and once again it fails. However, this time David does marry Michal, making him Saul's son-in-law.

However, David's being a part of the family didn't stop Saul's jealous pursuit to murder David. If you continue on in the text, you will find that Saul orders his soldiers to go to his daughter's house and kill her husband.

How's that for fatherly love! Saul treated his children horrendously! As we continue on, we see the same treatment given to Jonathan when he agreed to inform David what Saul's intentions were toward David. In this next verse, we read the story of Jonathan's confrontation with Saul.

Saul's anger flared up at Jonathan and he said to him, "You son of a perverse and rebellious woman! Don't I know that you have sided with the son of Jesse to your own shame and to the shame of the mother who bore you? As long as the son of Jesse lives on this earth, neither you nor your kingdom will be established. Now send someone to bring him to me, for he must die!" (1 Samuel 20:30–31).

How's that for the heart of a loving husband and father—he totally degrades and humiliates both Jonathan and his mother! If you think this is bad, it gets worse.

"Why should he be put to death? What has he done?" Jonathan asked his father. But Saul hurled his spear at him to kill him. Then Jonathan knew that his father intended to kill David.

Saul tried to murder his own son! He didn't care about Jonathan losing the throne. He didn't love his son. He didn't love Jonathan's mother. All Saul cared about was protecting himself and his kingship. He was not a family man. He was a self-centered, selfish man.

Jonathan was the complete opposite of his father. He was a man who loved his family and wanted to take care of them. He made sure they were safe and secure. How do I know this? We are told so in 1 Samuel 20:14–15.

When Jonathan went and told David that he needed to flee from Saul, he asked David to make a covenant with him.

> But show me unfailing kindness like the LORD's kindness as long as I live, so that I may not be killed, and do not ever cut off your kindness from my family—not even when the LORD has cut off every one of David's enemies from the face of the earth.

Jonathan is ensuring the safety of his family after David takes the throne. In those days, a new king would have all the former king's family killed so there would be no challenge to his authority. Jonathan made David promise him that he would not kill his family. He had the heart of a family man. He loved his family and put their safety and needs above his own. This is the heart of a *real* family man and it is the exact opposite heart that his father possessed.

I don't care what kind of an example you had of a father growing up. Even if you had no father, you can become a man who is deeply committed to his family. You are not doomed to become the same type of husband and father that you grew up with. You are not destined to cut and run. You can develop a godly heart that is committed to loving, honoring, and protecting your family. Jonathan did and so can you!

JONATHAN WAS FAITHFUL TO HIS JOB; SAUL WASN'T

The third area we are going to examine is the different hearts that Jonathan and Saul had in relation to their jobs. Jonathan grew up as a prince in the land of Israel. His father, Saul, was the first king of Israel. These were their jobs.

Saul was the ideal choice from a human perspective to be the first king of Israel. He stood head and shoulders above them all (1 Samuel 9:2). However, as we examine the way both men handled their jobs, it is clear that Jonathan was the bigger man.

God offered the world to Saul. Instead of allowing God to make him into a godly man and king, Saul began a downward spiral of fear, jealousy, and pride.

One of Saul's main jobs as king was to lead his men to war. Saul started out as a strong, effective military leader by winning a number of battles. However, as the sin in his life increased, his effectiveness at his job decreased.

I Samuel 13 tells us Saul was no longer leading Israel as an effective commander. He wouldn't even fight. At this point, Jonathan decided that he could no longer follow the ways of his evil father. He was fed up with his father's cowering and hiding. It was time for a new legacy!

That's when Jonathan manned up and took action. God's people were being oppressed by a heathen nation. As a true follower of God, he couldn't sit by and watch his father's indecisive behavior any longer. Jonathan grabbed his armor-bearer and said, "Let's go out and take a look at the Philistines' camp."

As Jonathan and his armor-bearer approached the camp, Jonathan became emboldened and decided to launch an attack. Let's look at what he says to his armor-bearer.

Jonathan said to his young armor-bearer, "Come, let's go over to the outpost of those uncircumcised men. Perhaps the LORD will act in our behalf. Nothing can hinder the LORD from saving, whether by many or by few."

"Do all that you have in mind," his armor-bearer said. "Go ahead; I am with you heart and soul."

Jonathan said, "Come on, then; we will cross over toward them and let them see us. If they say to us, 'Wait there until we come to you,' we will stay where we are and not go up to them. But if they say, 'Come up to us,' we will climb up, because that will be our sign that the LORD has given them into our hands" (1 Samuel 14:6–10).

What a heart! Jonathan boldly took the fight to the enemy. He was willing to do it alone if necessary. However, when you read the above passage, it is clear that Jonathan didn't consider himself alone. He knew God would be fighting right beside him. Saul may have stopped depending on God to fight for him, but Jonathan knew God could be counted on. He put himself in God's hands.

When Jonathan approached the Philistines, they called him up to them. Jonathan knew this was a sign that God was going to give him a mighty victory. Let's go back to the passage.

So Jonathan said to his armor-bearer, "Climb up after me; the LORD has given them into the hand of Israel."

Jonathan climbed up, using his hands and feet, with his armor-bearer right behind him. The Philistines fell before Jonathan, and his armor-bearer followed and killed behind him. In that first attack Jonathan and his armor-bearer killed some twenty men in an area of about half an acre.

Then panic struck the whole army—those in the camp and field, and those in the outposts and raiding parties—and the ground shook. It was a panic sent by God.

I love that! Jonathan stepped out in faith and attacked! He killed twenty men! He brought the boom! At this point, God stepped in and rewarded Jonathan's bold action by supernaturally jumping in and fighting for him. What was the result?

> *Then Saul and all his men assembled and went to the battle. They found the Philistines in total confusion, striking each other with their swords. Those Hebrews who had previously been with the Philistines and had gone up with them to their camp went over to the Israelites who were with Saul and Jonathan. When all the Israelites who had hidden in the hill country of Ephraim heard that the Philistines were on the run, they joined the battle in hot pursuit. So on that day the LORD saved Israel, and the battle moved on beyond Beth Aven.*

Because Jonathan decided not to take the same actions as his father, Israel experienced a great victory. Saul's actions caused the men of Israel to hide or desert. Jonathan inspired the entire nation to rise up and defend themselves. The end result was a victory and a relocation of the battle.

This was possible because Jonathan knew his responsibilities as the prince of Israel, and he boldly did them. He had a different heart than his dad and it came shining through in relation to his job.

I hope this chapter has given you hope that, like Jonathan, you are not doomed to be like your father and repeat his mistakes. During a very dark time in my life, the Holy Spirit used Jonathan's example to show me that, even though my dad only had a pretend relationship with God throughout his life, if I put the time and effort into it, I could have a genuine relationship with God and follow God wholeheartedly. In the life of Jonathan, I learned that even though my dad's choices destroyed most of his relationships, I could choose a different path and have healthy relationships. It challenged me to search my heart and my attitudes and start treating people—especially women—like Jesus did rather than the way my dad did.

Jonathan's example taught me that in every area of my life, I didn't have to follow the adage "Second verse, same as the first," but instead I could choose to create a different legacy—a godly legacy that was different than the one I'd seen demonstrated growing up. This challenge changed my life because it gave me hope that there was something to shoot for—a higher purpose to live my life. Like Jonathan, I could choose to create a new legacy of godliness.

The same is true for you. Unlike Amon, Manasseh's son who we mentioned in the first chapter, you can be a Jonathan and take action to be different. You can start a whole new legacy of godliness. With God's help and hard work, you can be a godly man, free from the chains of your generational sins. You are not doomed to live the same life as your father. You can become your own man. You can develop your own legacy!

You can develop a heart that loves and serves God and is committed to submitting to his will. You can begin a new generational pattern of godliness, one in which your children can have pride and want to follow. You can be a godly man who is dedicated to his life's work. You can be known as a worker who is good, loyal, and dependable. There is no area of your life that can't develop the heart of a godly man and succeed. It will take hard work and a willingness to make changes, but in the end it will be worth it. You can get started today.

Dear heavenly Father, you know the example I had growing up. You have seen the sins, the mistakes, the bad decisions, and the pain. I don't want to go down the same path of destruction which I have seen my father go down. Please show me any way I am like my father and not like you. Give me clear direction on how to change. Help me to develop a heart that is totally submitted to your will.

Help me to become a man that not only I can be proud of, but a man that you and my children can be proud of. Help me as I pursue becoming a godly man. In Jesus' name, amen.

LEGACY CHALLENGES

1. Make a list of all the areas in which you do not want to follow your father.

2. Then develop a battle plan to make changes to become different.

EXTREME LEGACY CHALLENGES

If possible, discuss with your dad or other family members why your father did what he did or is the way he is. Don't be judgmental or hard on him. Be gentle and approach it from the point that you just want to understand why. This information can help you forgive your dad. This will allow you to be free to pursue a new life course.

GROUP STUDY QUESTIONS

1. What is your relationship with your father like?

2. Was there a point when you found out that your father wasn't what you thought he was? Do you want to turn out like your dad?

3. What actions must stop and what changes must happen so that you don't end up like your dad?

4. Did your father have a relationship with God? How did this affect your view of God?

5. Was your father a family man? Did he put his family's needs first?

6. What was your father's work ethic like? How did he view his job? How did this affect your view of work?

7. In the extreme homework, forgiving your father is discussed. Why is this important?

8. How can we as a group work together to start new legacies of godliness?

3

THE JOSHUA LEGACY

STANDING STRONG
AND COURAGEOUS

I remember it like it was yesterday! I was eighteen years old, away from home for the first time as I began my freshman year of college. I was scared to death! I have always struggled with fear controlling my life, but this was different. I was out of my element completely!

It wasn't like I didn't know anyone at the college. My sister was a senior during my freshman year, so I knew some of her friends. So I had this comfort blanket to rely on, but still, I felt the enormity of change in my life.

Then it happened. Some of the guys in my dorm that I had met at orientation asked me to come with them dam jumping. Now, you have to understand, I am not an adventurous person by nature. I am cautious and careful. I grew up with a lot of fear issues because of my dad's abuse. But that day, something inside of me said I needed to step up and conquer my fears if I was going to survive four years of college. So I accepted their offer.

As we drove toward the dam, I was literally shaking. I was scared to death. My fear was in no way alleviated when they told me to keep my eyes out for cops, because they frowned upon the college students jumping off the dam. Technically, it wasn't completely legal, but all the cops could do was ticket you for parking along the side of the road. I wanted to go straight back to the car and drive back to campus! However, there were already about twenty to thirty other students there, so I couldn't back out now!

I will never forget how I felt standing on the edge of the rocks, preparing to jump thousands of feet to my death! (Okay, it was only about thirty feet, but to me it seemed WAY higher!) Somehow, I found the strength to run up and make the leap!

I will NEVER forget the feeling as my fear was replaced by this amazing feeling of freedom and excitement as gravity pulled me to the water. I am sure I was screaming like a little girl the whole way down, but, when I resurfaced from the water, I felt such a sense of victory and freedom! I had conquered a fear! I had survived! (By the way, after we jumped about five more times, a cop did come and he ticketed the driver!)

IN LIFE, FEAR KEEPS YOU FROM MOVING FORWARD, WHILE COURAGE BRINGS YOU VICTORY.

This was just the first of many times I have had to step to the edge of a seemingly mile-high cliff and jump, pushing my fear aside to do what God was calling me to do. I had to learn that, in life, fear keeps you from moving forward, while courage brings you victory. The next man we are going to study provides an excellent example of how to overcome fear and become strong and courageous.

I am very excited about this chapter! We are going to look at one of my favorite men in the Bible, Joshua. Joshua was an incredible man.

We first read about Joshua in Exodus 17. However, Joshua's story begins way before the Bible mentions him.

Joshua was born in very difficult circumstances. He was a slave and a son of a slave. This is important to remember. He is heralded as the great leader who led the Israelites into the Promised Land, but he was born as a slave.

Joshua's father's name was Nun. Nun was a slave in Egypt, living a life of forced labor under Pharaoh. We see Nun's trust in God to bring his people out of slavery by the name he gave his son, Hoshea, which means "Salvation." Later, it was changed to Joshua. Nun was a man of vision who felt salvation needed to come to the next generation, which is exactly what happened.

In the book of Exodus, we read that God called Moses to lead his people out of bondage in Egypt. After God performed many supernatural acts (which are horribly reenacted in all Bible movies, just sayin'), the Pharaoh let the Israelites go. Joshua saw the mighty deliverance of the Israelites from Egypt and the parting of the Red Sea. He witnessed first-hand the destruction of Pharaoh and his army as the Red Sea came pouring back down on them. Joshua learned that the power of God was real, and that he used it to help his people. He learned as a young man that when it is God's timing to act on our behalf, **God holds nothing back.**

Joshua participated in the first Passover celebration.

He was one of the men circumcised in Exodus 13.

He saw the pillar of fire and the cloud that led the people of Israel on the safest route out of Egypt (Exodus 13:17–18).

He ate the manna and he drank from the rock (Exodus 16).

Joshua experienced firsthand the power and deliverance of his people from oppression and captivity. Trusting God and following him with courage should have been no problem for Joshua.

The book of Exodus shows Moses took Joshua and made him his aide. How's that for an intern program, working directly under the great Moses!

Moses changed Hoshea's name to Joshua, which means "Jehovah is Salvation." The changing of a name in biblical times showed that Moses had formed a father-like relationship with Joshua. God used Moses to prepare young Joshua for the calling that was placed on his life. Joshua needed to know that the coming events were not of his own doing. They were the actions of Jehovah saving his people.

Joshua experienced miracles we can only dream of experiencing. However, his years as a slave had left a mark on his life. Being beaten down and owned by another man apparently left Joshua feeling timid and fearful. He managed to overcome it to a degree as Moses' aide. After all, the buck stopped with Moses; there was security in being second in command. However, as we turn to the book of Joshua (the following verses are from the NKJV), we see that Joshua once and for all had to face his biggest enemy in order to become the man God called him to be.

MOSES WAS DEAD, TO BEGIN WITH

After the death of Moses the servant of the Lord, *it came to pass that the* Lord *spoke to Joshua the son of Nun, Moses' assistant.*

Moses, the great leader of the nation of Israel, has died. Joshua is now the leader of the people of Israel. As leader, his chief responsibility is to lead the people of Israel into war against their enemies. Joshua is an experienced fighter. He had led the Israelite army in the past when the nation came under attack. However, in the past he was just following orders. Now he had to be the one giving the orders and sending other men off to fight and maybe die.

The Lord spoke to Joshua the son of Nun, Moses' assistant, saying: "Moses My servant is dead. Now therefore, arise, go over this Jordan, you and all this people, to the land which I am giving to them—the children of Israel. Every place that the sole of your foot will tread upon I have given you, as I said to Moses. From the wilderness and this Lebanon as far as the great river, the River Euphrates, all the land of the Hittites, and to the Great Sea toward the going down of the sun, shall be your territory. No man shall be able to stand before you all the days of your life; as I was with Moses, so I will be with you. I will not leave you nor forsake you.

Joshua was well aware of the promises God had given to Moses. He knew God had promised to give them back their land. He knew in the past God had helped the nation win battles under Moses, and he could now be certain that God would help him in the same way.

There must have been a part of Joshua that felt inadequate and downright fearful to step into the role of leading the nation of Israel. It is one thing to follow Moses' orders and have Moses answer to God. But now Moses was gone, and the buck stopped with Joshua. How could he, a former slave who spent his whole life following someone else's orders, now lead? God saw this fear inside of Joshua and spoke words of life and hope to him.

Be strong and of good courage, for to this people you shall divide as an inheritance the land which I swore to their fathers to give them. Only be strong and very courageous, that you may observe to do according to all the law which Moses My servant commanded you; do not turn from it to the right hand or to the left, that you may prosper wherever you go. This Book of the Law shall not depart from your mouth, but you shall meditate in it day and night, that you may observe to do according to all that is written in it. For then you will make your way prosperous, and then you will have good success. Have I not commanded you? Be strong and of

*good courage; do not be afraid, nor be dismayed, for the LORD your
God is with you wherever you go.*

What words of strength and encouragement given to Joshua by
God! God was guaranteeing Joshua victory and success. He is promised that his ways would prosper. God guaranteed him success! However, he required one thing of Joshua. Three different times, God commands Joshua to be strong and courageous!

The choice was now before Joshua. He is guaranteed success and
victory by God. All he had to do was get up, walk to the edge of his
dam, and find the courage and strength to take the million-foot leap
(yes, it gets higher every time I tell it!) and follow God. Did he do it?

*So Joshua ordered the officers of the people: "Go through the camp
and tell the people, 'Get your provisions ready. Three days from
now you will cross the Jordan here to go in and take possession of
the land the LORD your God is
giving you for your own.'"*

**EVERY MAN HAS A CALL
ON HIS LIFE. GOD HAS
CALLED US ALL
TO BE STRONG AND
COURAGEOUS!**

With a supernatural courage
and resolve, Joshua got up, and
proclaimed to the people of Israel,
"Mount up, it's time to stop griev-
ing and start moving forward!"
With absolute resolve and courage,
Joshua stood and obeyed God's
commands. He conquered his fears and walked into the calling God
had for him. Guys, we need to do the same.

Every man has a call on his life. God has called us all to be strong
and courageous. Just like he did with Joshua, he calls us to boldly go
where he leads, and follow his commands.

God is calling us as his men to get some courage, stand up, and fight! He calls us to be men committed to obeying him and the principles in his Word.

Remember, God told Joshua to not let the Book of the Law depart from him. We need to make sure, as we step into the place God called us, that we do it according to his Word. Trust me, in the world in which we live, this is vitally important. Why?

Because in today's society, men are under attack. The enemy has placed his bull's eye squarely on our backs. He knows as go the men, so goes a nation. He is trying to devalue men. He is feminizing men.

Our culture is actively redefining men. The world says men are selfish, only out for themselves.

They say you live to play and be irresponsible, you only work to have money to play.

They say you are too stupid to lead a family.

They say you don't care about family. They believe you will turn your back and abandon your family.

Men are seen as having no morals or convictions. We are all just playboys chasing after any and all women. A real man in society is a man who is with a different woman each night. You can't stay faithful to one woman for the rest of your life.

You have been redefined as detatched figures who cannot feel or express emotions.

You have been declared uninterested in God. You hate to learn and grow. You won't read the Bible or pray. You have no interest in being in a men's group. You're not qualified to lead in your church.

According to today's culture, you have no ability to manage money or be financially responsible. You only use money for play and self-gratification.

Guys, the enemy is attacking and devaluing us at every turn. Unfortunately, his lies are being seen as fact, and as a result, the decline in men is resulting in a decline in our society. We are on the brink of facing God's judgment as a nation. Once again, God is looking for strong and courageous men who will stand up and say, "I WILL STAND! I will do it God's way, I will make a difference!"

We need to courageously declare, "I am going to be the head of my family. Even if men all around me desert their family, I am committed to standing beside my family!"

GOD IS LOOKING FOR STRONG MEN! HE IS LOOKING FOR MEN WITH COURAGE! WILL YOU WALK TO THE CLIFF AND FIND STRENGTH TO LEAP INTO GOD'S CALLING ON YOUR LIFE?

With courage we must proclaim, "I am committed to working hard and providing for my family. Even if everyone around me uses their money for their own selfish gain, I will be a good steward and use it to provide for my family and to invest in God's kingdom."

We must boldly say to the world around us, "I am committed to being a one-woman man. I will never cheat on my wife. I have eyes only for her." If you are single, then commit to standing pure and abstaining until you're married. Show the world men can stand pure and not be womanizers.

We can all stand for God and declare, "I am a strong and confident man, confident enough to express emotions when I feel them. I will not fall into the world's trap of saying I have no emotions or feelings. I will express my feelings like a mature, godly man, while not allowing my emotions to overflow in an unhealthy way."

Guys, we need to man up and courageously take a stand for God. We must declare we are men who love God's Word, who make it a priority, and who strive to live by his commandments. We will follow God wholeheartedly.

We will submit to him. We will take our place in the church and give to others instead of always taking. We will have active, thriving men's ministries, not designed around taking from each other, but designed around giving to each other and the community while providing help and support to each other in our spiritual battles.

Guys, God is looking for strong men! He is looking for men with courage! Will you walk to the cliff and find the strength to leap into God's calling on your life?

There have been times in my life when I needed to decide if I would be strong and courageous and follow God. I remember the day I realized I was following my father's sinful legacy instead of creating a godly legacy. I had to decide to stand and say, *No more: I am going to do things God's way.*

I remember when God called me to once again leap off the edge by starting Mantour Ministries. God spoke to me to start holding men's conferences throughout the state, to stand in the gap and do what needed to be done.

Quite honestly, when God started putting this vision on my heart, it was terrifying.

Who was I to stand up and say, "More needs to be done, let me do it!"

I was terrified to approach our district men's director and tell him my vision. It would be very understandable for him to take my vision as an attack on his leadership. It was not my heart at all, but if I miscommunicated my heart, it could have gone really, really badly.

That's when I decided that this wasn't happening, no way no how!

Then a few weeks a later, I was listening to a sermon by Pastor Choco. In the message, he said something to the effect of, "If God is calling you to do something as a minister and you're not doing it because of fear, than you have no business being in ministry."

It was like he stuck a knife through my heart! God had called me to start Mantour conferences, but I was too afraid to obey.

Once again, I had to choose to stand and courageously jump off the cliff and follow his lead. I needed to find the courage to stand and do something that needed to be done. So I made the appointment with the men's director and shared my heart.

The rest is history. Thankfully, he saw my heart and discerned I was following God and offered to be my coach as we got started. Rather than being rejected, I was offered support, wisdom, and all the advice that I needed.

But I never would have known this, started Mantour Ministries, or even published this book if I hadn't jumped off this cliff to go where God was leading me.

That's the Joshua legacy: standing strong and courageous—boldly following God despite your fear.

It's like one of the great theologians of our time, John Wayne, once said, "Courage is being scared to death, but saddling up anyway."

Eddie Rickenbacker, American fighter ace in World War I and Medal of Honor recipient, once said "Courage is doing what you are afraid to do. There can be no courage unless you are scared."

A man of God faces his fear and does what needs doing—that is courage!

Joshua's legacy is one of a man who courageously followed God's lead and conquered all the territory God had promised the nation of Israel. No enemy could stand against Joshua and Israel whenever they obeyed God's commands with courage and strength.

A man can never realize his full potential in God's kingdom until he comes to the place where he is willing to conquer his fears and be strong and courageous. Our world is crying out for men who will be strong and courageous! The question is, *Will you be that man?*

Will you begin to live your life with God with strength and courage? Will you make it your life's goal to follow God wherever he sends you, to do whatever he asks you to do, no matter how big or overwhelming the job may be? If so, you are well on your way to developing the legacy of a strong and courageous man!

Dear heavenly Father, you know my heart. You know my desire to follow you completely. However, you also see my fears, my weaknesses, and my insecurities. Please give me a supernatural strength, a divine courage, to boldly follow wherever you lead me and to do whatever you ask me to do.

Father, I admit my natural tendency is not to throw caution to wind or to jump off the cliff. However, I know if you're leading me off the cliff, I have no choice but to follow. Please make me strong and courageous! Give me courage to conquer my fears today. In Jesus' name, amen!

LEGACY CHALLENGES

God told Joshua that part of being strong and courageous was following the commands found in the Word of God, no matter what the cost. The only way to know God's Word is to read God's Word, so commit to a daily Bible reading plan. Places like Biblegateway.com have Bible reading plans they will send you daily via e-mail. Utilize such a plan so you can begin hiding God's Word in your heart.

EXTREME LEGACY CHALLENGES

Ask yourself, "What is one thing I can do for God's kingdom that I am too scared to do I my own strength?"

Then find a way to do it. Examples may be starting a ministry at your church, witnessing more, stepping into a leadership position at church, etc.

47

GROUP STUDY QUESTIONS

1. What is your cliff, the thing God is asking you to courageously step up and do for him?

2. Has fear kept you from doing something God has asked you to do? Why?

3. What would be accomplished for the kingdom of God if you overcame this fear?

4. How can being strong and courageous make a difference in your family?

5. How can being strong and courageous make a difference in your church?

6. How can being strong and courageous make a difference in your community?

7. How can we as a group work together to become strong and courageous men?

4

THE PHINEHAS LEGACY

BEING A MAN OF ZEAL

Did you have a hero when you were child? Most of us did. For some, it was the athletic superstar of his day, while others loved the soldier or the cowboy from the movies. For me, it was the Lone Ranger. I was obsessed! I had the toy guns, the hat, the mask, and even plastic silver bullets. I loved watching this masked hero and his brave friend, Tonto, as they fought to uphold integrity and honesty in the Old West. (Let me clarify that I am talking about the REAL Lone Ranger, not the awful version that hit theatres a few years back!)

Each episode ended the same way.

The Lone Ranger would leave his famous silver bullet with whoever he had helped. When he left, someone would always ask, "Who was that masked man?" Someone else would always answer, "Why, he is the Lone Ranger!" Then they would wave goodbye as the Lone Ranger and Tonto rode off to the glorious cheer of "Hi-Yo, Silver! Away!"

While most of us had heroes as children, few of us have them as adults. We have become jaded and proud. We no longer seek men to look up to and model ourselves after. I think this is sad. I feel we all need to find men we can look to as heroes, and the Bible is full of heroic men.

Today, as we turn together to Numbers 25, I want to introduce you to one of my heroes. His name is Phinehas. Phinehas is the perfect man to demonstrate how to develop a legacy of zeal and become a man who is willing to do whatever it takes kill the sins in our lives.

Who is Phinehas? Phinehas was the grandson of Moses' brother Aaron, the high priest. Like Joshua, Phinehas lived through the miracles when Israel was freed from Egyptian slavery.

Most people don't know that the story of Phinehas actually begins with another popular Bible story—the tale of Balaam and his talking donkey. In the last chapter, we discussed how Joshua led the war party against the Amalekites. After this battle, Israel fought and conquered the areas just outside the Promised Land. Next, they prepared the battle plan for the conquest of the land God promised them. This fact didn't go unnoticed by the king of Moab, whose land was just inside the area Israel was planning to invade.

In Deuteronomy 2:9 we read:

Then the LORD said to me, "Do not harass the Moabites or provoke them to war, for I will not give you any part of their land. I have given Ar to the descendants of Lot as a possession."

The people of Israel were forbidden to attack or harm Moab. However, the king of Moab did not know this fact. Because he was afraid of Israel and their military might, Balak, the king of Moab, hired Balaam, a prophet, to come and proclaim a curse on the nation of Israel.

When Balaam received the king's request and the offer of a huge financial windfall, he immediately wanted to go. As Balaam proceeded on the long trek to Moab, he is stopped and warned not to curse Israel.

This is done through the miraculous phenomenon of having his donkey speak to him. (Really cool story, I'll resist the many obvious jokes!) He is told that if he insisted on going, he may only say what God tells him to say.

When Balaam arrives, he goes to view the Israelite's camp and tries to speak his curse, but the only thing God allowed him to do was bless the Israelites.

Balak, furious at Balaam's blessing, demanded he try again.

The same thing happened each time he tried to curse Israel. Finally, unable to bring a curse upon the people of Israel, an exasperated Balaam taught the Moabites how to provoke the Lord's anger against Israel. This is where our story involving Phinehas begins.

> *While Israel was staying in Shittim, the men began to indulge in sexual immorality with Moabite women, who invited them to the sacrifices to their gods. The people ate the sacrificial meal and bowed down before these gods. So Israel yoked themselves to the Baal of Peor. And the LORD's anger burned against them (Numbers 25:1–3).*

This passage describes Baalam's evil plot. He taught the Moabites how to trap the Israelites and cause a breech between them and God. The plan was simple: Get the Moabite women to seduce the Israelite men and cause them to participate in the sensual Moabite religious system.

The Israelite men fell into their trap. As a result, God's anger was aroused against the entire Israelite community.

> *The LORD said to Moses, "Take all the leaders of these people, kill them and expose them in broad daylight before the LORD, so that the LORD's fierce anger may turn away from Israel."*
>
> *So Moses said to Israel's judges, "Each of you must put to death those of your people who have yoked themselves to the Baal of Peor.*

God's command to Moses was clear: kill the sinners and remove the sin from the camp. Anyone who worshiped false gods with the women was to be killed.

This message is important for all men today. God wants us to destroy all the sin in our lives so we can become holy men, devoted solely to the Lord. We can't entertain it or ignore it, we must annihilate it! Only then can we move forward and obtain the great things God promises us.

> **GOD WANTS US TO DESTROY ALL THE SIN IN OUR LIVES SO WE CAN BECOME HOLY MEN, DEVOTED SOLELY TO HIM.**

Let's get back to the story. Moses and the children of Israel took the action necessary to remove the sin from among the people. The entire congregation was rededicated to God. They learned a hard lesson and were back on track. You would think they would never want to sin with the other nations again. Problem solved; lesson learned.

Not quite! I wish the story ended that way, but as we continue on we see the opposite.

Then an Israelite man brought into the camp a Midianite woman right before the eyes of Moses and the whole assembly of Israel while they were weeping at the entrance to the tent of meeting.

Can you believe it? What shameless audacity and rebellion against the holiness of God! This man, in direct defiance and rebellion to God, took his Midianite girlfriend, the daughter of the head Midianite priest, into the tent of meeting!

In the holy presence of God, they engaged in a sexual embrace in the manner of Baal worship! If this wasn't offensive enough, he did it on the day that Israel was trying to get right with God and remove the sin from their lives.

This was a heinous act! It was rebellion against the very nature of God! This sin rivals the rebellious action of Satan which caused him to get thrown out of heaven!

If God wasn't already angry with the nation of Israel and willing to destroy them, he surely was now! Immediate action needed to be taken.

This is where we first meet Phinehas. He demonstrates that a godly man is passionate for God and will do whatever is necessary to remove sin from his life. He was a man of zeal!

WE MUST HAVE A PASSION TO DESTROY SIN BEFORE IT DESTROYS US

When Phinehas son of Eleazar, the son of Aaron, the priest, saw this, he left the assembly, took a spear in his hand and followed the Israelite into the tent. He drove the spear into both of them, right through the Israelite man and into the woman's stomach. Then the plague against the Israelites was stopped; but those who died in the plague numbered 24,000.

Phinehas brought the BOOM! I love this man! After seeing the horrific display of defiance against God, he was immediately filled with righteous, holy indignation.

We see that God's wrath was already underway because it mentions a plague. Phinehas knew that his life, as well as the lives of the rest of God's children, was in grave danger. He knew God's holiness was under direct attack. Action needed to be taken!

Phinehas loved God and his nation. He couldn't stand by and let this pompous, rebellious traitor bring judgment on his people. So he mans up, grabs a spear, runs up to the rebellious couple, and slams his spear directly though them both while they were having sex in God's holy tent!

This is a man of God! He loves God and so desires God's presence that he will kill any sin that threatens to get in the way!

I love the description of Phinehas' actions: He was overcome with righteous anger. It took tremendous strength to do what he did! Phinehas had a tremendous, supernatural strength of character, bound and formed around an intense desire to show honor and respect to God.

> **PHINEHAS HAD A TREMENDOUS, SUPERNATURAL STRENGTH OF CHARACTER, BOUND AND FORMED AROUND AN INTENSE DESIRE TO SHOW HONOR AND RESPECT TO GOD.**

What was this strength? We continue on the story to see how God himself describes it.

The LORD said to Moses, "Phinehas son of Eleazar, the son of Aaron, the priest, has turned my anger away from the Israelites. Since he was as zealous for my honor among them as I am, I did not put an end to them in my zeal. Therefore tell him I am making my covenant of peace with him. He and his descendants will have a covenant of a lasting priesthood, because he was zealous for the honor of his God and made atonement for the Israelites."

How cool is it to have God himself write your legacy!

God declared that Phinehas was *"zealous for my honor."*

What exactly does this mean? According to Webster's dictionary, *zeal* means "fervor for a person, cause, or object; eager desire or endeavour; enthusiastic; diligence; ardor."

Phinehas had an eager desire, fervor, to see the holiness of God defended. The original Hebrew word used here is *qana*, which means to be jealous or envious.

The idea is that Phinehas loved God so much that he was jealous for God's sake. He hated that this man was in essence cheating on God. He felt the same pain that God was feeling and he took action to put an end to it.

This character trait is essential in a godly man. We must hate evil. We cannot tolerate it. We must take appropriate action to deal with the evil around us. This action by Phinehas was appropriate to the circumstances.

This is the Phineas legacy: A godly man has a zeal for holiness.

Whatever it takes, he will destroy the sin.

This is important, given the "freedom in Christ" atmosphere that exists in today's world. Too many sins are being tolerated and too much compromise is taking place because people feel they have the right to do what they want because they have freedom in Christ. They use the words of Paul as a free pass to throw off holiness. They ignore the warning of Paul that we should not use his words as an excuse to sin. Some have lost a true sense of the holiness of God. It is time we follow the words found in the book of 1 Peter and become holy as God is holy.

We must have a passion to be holy and take appropriate action against sin. Such a man receives a blessing from God.

God said to Phinehas,

> *I am making my covenant of peace with him. He and his descendants will have a covenant of a lasting priesthood, because he was zealous for the honor of his God and made atonement for the Israelites.*

IT IS TIME WE FOLLOW THE WORDS FOUND IN THE BOOK OF 1 PETER AND BECOME HOLY AS GOD IS HOLY.

God was thrilled with Phinehas' action. He rewarded him with the promise that for all of eternity, Phinehas' descendants would be his priests. This promise will extend even through the millennial reign of Christ. That is a long time! God will not fail to take care of those who take care of his reputation.

A ZEALOUS MAN WILL SEE HIS SIN AS AN OFFENSE AGAINST THE HOLINESS OF GOD.

You may be thinking, "I agree that a truly godly man is zealous for God and needs to take action against sin, but do you really think it is okay to go around driving spears through people?"

My answer to you is, "Duh! Of course it is not okay."

We have to understand one thing: the Bible is both a literal and a spiritual book. The accounts in the Bible were all true stories that happened to real people. However, there is also spiritual imagery of how a believer should live.

God wants us to kill unholiness and sin. This mostly involves the sin in our lives. It is our duty to discern the sin living inside of us. Then we, like Phinehas, must show it no mercy. It must be dealt with quickly.

I remember a time when I had to attack such an area of sin. God showed me that I had a problem with telling the truth. When push came to shove, I would lie to avoid getting in trouble. I could look you square in the eye and lie to your face without blinking. It was a horrible sin inside of me that was in direct opposition to the ways of God, who is pure truth and holiness. I had to change. I had to destroy this sin in my life.

As a result, God required me to speak nothing but truth. If I spoke something that was not 100 percent accurate, I would have to go back and correct it. I was so zealous that I would correct the most minute details. I would correct statements, even if it was a simple as saying something "took me five minutes" and it actually took me six.

At one point, the Holy Spirit reminded me of a time I had lied a few years earlier while in college to avoid paying a fine. He required me to write the college a letter asking forgiveness, and to include the money for the fine. After going to such extremes, you get tired of the embarrassment and burden of correcting yourself and you form the new habit of speaking the truth. I realized the seriousness of my lying and took my spear and killed it.

Another area where I had to grab my spear was in my driving habits. I always drove fast. Going 80–90 miles per hour on a highway was common for me. I would pass cars whether or not it was a passing zone.

One day God showed me that this was a sin. I was not submitting to the speed limit laws and the governing authorities over me. Now I make myself obey the speed limit, even when it seems ridiculous. It was hard, but it was sin and it had to go. These are just a few examples of the many sins God has made me face and learn to spear to death.

A zealous man will see his sin as an offense against the holiness of God. Like Phinehas, he will bring the boom and drive a spear through it with all the vigor he possesses because he wants to become as godly a man as possible.

The chief times in life when you will need to "spear" sin is when you discover it in your *own* life. It will be as revolting to you to see sin in your "tabernacle" as it was for Phinehas to see the sin in his tabernacle.

What about you? What areas of sin do you still face in your life?

You need to be a godly man and acknowledge your sin.

Then be like Phinehas and be brutal. Show it no mercy.

I encourage you to grab your spear, face your sin, and destroy it with all your might. It is what Phinehas did, and it is what any man who longs to have a deep, zealous relationship with God would do. When you do, you are developing the legacy of a man of zeal, and a man of zeal can change the world!

> *Dear heavenly Father, please forgive me for any time I have been ashamed to stand against evil or have looked the other way. From this day forward, I want to be a man like Phinehas who will stand up and fight against sin in my life. Show me the areas of sin and give me strength and boldness as I face them. I want to destroy my sin and enter into a deeper relationship with you. In Jesus' name, amen.*

LEGACY CHALLENGES

1. Ask the Holy Spirit to show you areas of sin that stand between you and God.

2. Make a list and repent of the sins.

3. Stop doing the sin and change your behavior.

EXTREME LEGACY CHALLENGES

In this chapter, I mentioned that God required me to mail a check and ask forgiveness from my college in order to break the habit of lying. Is there sin in your life that you need to make restitution for? Do it. Ask the Holy Spirit how you could make it right. It may be embarrassing, but it is the fastest way to destroy the sin in your life.

GROUP STUDY QUESTIONS

1. Do you understand why we need a zeal for God?

2. Do you believe you have a freedom in Christ to sin, or do you believe you need to pursue holiness?

3. Are there areas of sin in your life that you tolerate?

4. How can you go about removing these sins from your life?

5. How can we as a group help you kill the areas of sin in your life?

6. How can we as a group work together to ensure compromise doesn't creep into our men's group? Our families? Our church?

5

——◆——

THE CALEB LEGACY

STARTING STRONG, FINISHING WELL

Ever since my mom passed away five years ago, I often remember conversations we had together, recalling her words of wisdom, laughing inside at her jokes, and mentally reliving common experiences we had together. Recently, I was thinking about a conversation I had with my mom and my sister shortly before my mom passed away.

During this conversation, my sister made reference to how controlling and abusive someone in our lives had been. I hadn't thought about it in years. As she spoke, the only thought that went through my mind was, *I am so glad to be free of that. I am never going back under that bondage.* The funny thing was that while I was thinking these words, my mom interrupted my thoughts by saying the exact same words.

This is the attitude we should have when God sets us free from the bondage in our lives. We should be repulsed by our past and never want to go back. We should be grateful for the freedom, and seek to serve God with everything in us. As a result, we will desire to completely destroy our enemies.

In the last two chapters, we learned that living free of bondage allows us to develop a heart for God. This was demonstrated through the life of Joshua. Also, we learned how to remove sin in our lives so we can be free to serve God. Phinehas showed us how to completely kill these sins.

In this chapter, we are going to learn how to be men who are wholeheartedly devoted to God. I can't think of a better man than Caleb to teach us this lesson. He is the perfect demonstration of a man who was so grateful to be set free that he served God wholeheartedly and ensured his freedom by defeating his enemies. That was Caleb's legacy.

It is important to realize one thing about Caleb: like Joshua and Phineas, he was born a slave in Egypt. He had no freedom to live his life the way he wanted. He was owned by someone else. They controlled him. They held him down. He was beaten and abused. However, through the power of God, Caleb was set free!

We are all in the same situation. We are all Calebs, born into slavery. It is slavery to sin, Satan, and his kingdom. However, God has given us a way to be free through Jesus Christ. Accepting him as our Savior is the first step of our freedom.

God called Caleb out of slavery in Egypt and Caleb wholeheartedly accepted. This was Caleb's first step toward freedom. He hated Egypt and slavery and he was never going back! This is the key to Caleb's life.

Once Caleb had his freedom, he never allowed himself to be *free* because he was so grateful to God; he made himself God's *servant*. God was his new Master and he was never going back to his old life again!

Caleb devoted his whole heart, body, mind, and soul to God. It was the will of God that mattered to Caleb! He had the opportunity to develop into the man God wanted him to become. He could experience new ways of living, learn new skills, stretch his knowledge and abilities. He was both grateful to God and excited about what lay ahead.

We need to learn this lesson from Caleb so we can be free.

We must be grateful to God for our freedom. Out of that gratitude, we must be willing to serve God wholeheartedly. Our life's mission, a legacy we should be pursuing, is to serve God wholeheartedly and not to go back to our old life.

The first time we read about Caleb is in Numbers 13–14. This is one of the coolest passages in the Bible. It is James Bond meets the Dirty Dozen.

In these verses, we see twelve men going on the ultimate spy mission. Take a minute and read these chapters. Caleb was chosen to be one of twelve men assigned by Moses to spy out the land of Canaan. It was a new opportunity for him. Caleb found himself with an exciting chance to repay God in a small way for everything God did for him.

> **WE MUST BE GRATEFUL TO GOD FOR OUR FREEDOM. OUT OF THAT GRATITUDE, WE MUST BE WILLING TO SERVE GOD WHOLE-HEARTEDLY.**

Caleb, along with Joshua and ten other men, set out on the great spying mission. Their mission, should they choose to accept it, was to gather information that would help Moses prepare the battle plan for taking the Promised Land. You almost wonder if a tape self-destructed after receiving their orders from Moses!

The group spent forty days traveling through Canaan. They studied the layout of the land and the people. They took note of the weak and strong points. They looked for ways to gain the upper hand as they began their conquest to inherit their new promised home.

After forty days, Caleb and the other spies returned to give their report to Moses. They relayed the great news that the land was rich and plentiful. As proof, they showed them a cluster of grapes they brought back with them. This may seem like no big deal, however, it took two men to carry one cluster of grapes! This was one great place they were heading toward!

You would expect the spies to be excited and anxious to begin their military campaign. However, ten of the spies had other ideas. Let's look at Numbers 13:27–29:

> *They gave Moses this account: "We went into the land to which you sent us, and it does flow with milk and honey! Here is its fruit. But the people who live there are powerful, and the cities are fortified and very large. We even saw descendants of Anak there. The Amalekites live in the Negev; the Hittites, Jebusites and Amorites live in the hill country; and the Canaanites live near the sea and along the Jordan."*

Can you believe this? These ten men are discouraging Moses and the nation from going and conquering their promised territory! Not only that, but they are purposely trying to fill the people with fear.

We see this through their description of the descendants of Anak, a race of people who had settled in Palestine before the Canaanites took possession. These were unusually large people, probably the forefathers of men like Goliath of Gath seen in 1 Samuel. Also, they refer to the Nephilim, a race of giants described briefly in Genesis 6:4.

Their report and description of the Nephilim had its desired effect, because panic spread through the camp. At this point, we see Caleb shine through.

> *Then Caleb silenced the people before Moses and said, "We should go up and take possession of the land, for we can certainly do it."*

What a statement of faith! Here is a man, who in the middle of the bad report, stands up and says, "We can do this!" Caleb spoke the words of a man who believed that God would fulfill his promise and give them the land. He had full confidence in God and was willing to follow him no matter what. Unfortunately, his feelings weren't shared by the rest of the camp.

That night all the members of the community raised their voices and wept aloud. All the Israelites grumbled against Moses and Aaron, and the whole assembly said to them, "If only we had died in Egypt! Or in this wilderness! Why is the LORD bringing us to this land only to let us fall by the sword? Our wives and children will be taken as plunder. Wouldn't it be better for us to go back to Egypt?" And they said to each other, "We should choose a leader and go back to Egypt" (Numbers 14:1–4).

These words sent Caleb into action. He was not about to go back to Egypt and become a slave again! He didn't care what trials or troubles lay ahead. He wasn't concerned about facing a stronger army. He knew God set them free and he was grateful to God for his freedom. NO ONE was making him go back again!

Joshua son of Nun and Caleb son of Jephunneh, who were among those who had explored the land, tore their clothes and said to the entire Israelite assembly, "The land we passed through and explored is exceedingly good. If the LORD is pleased with us, he will lead us into that land, a land flowing with milk and honey, and will give it to us. Only do not rebel against the LORD. And do not be afraid of the people of the land, because we will devour them. Their protection is gone, but the LORD is with us. Do not be afraid of them."

This is one of the ultimate rally speeches in history! It puts Braveheart's William Wallace to shame! This is the real deal! With a heart full of love and devotion to God, Caleb and Joshua stood up and fought for the God they gratefully served. No one was making them go back!

They knew the nation was in great sin and rebellion against the God they loved, and they took action to try and end it. They were not going to quit on God. They were moving forward with or without the rest of the people!

Of course, their speech rallied the crowd, and the entire nation cried out, "We can do it! God will give us the victory!" WRONG!

CALEB WOULD RATHER DIE THAN GO BACK TO THE PLACE FROM WHICH HE HAD BEEN FREED.

But the whole assembly talked about stoning them.

What?! Instead of listening and moving forward with God, the nation wanted to kill Joshua and Caleb!

It is obvious from the passage the whole assembly wanted them dead. This included friends, the men they had previously fought side by side with in the heat of battle.

However, not even the threat of death could stop Caleb. He would rather die than go back to the place from which he had been freed. He would rather lose relationships than lose the God that mattered more to him than anyone or anything else. This is the heart of devotion that characterized the life and legacy of Caleb. As you continue the passage, you see that Caleb's faith was rewarded by God.

"Not one of you will enter the land I swore with uplifted hand to make your home, except Caleb son of Jephunneh and Joshua son of Nun. As for your children that you said would be taken as plunder, I will bring them in to enjoy the land you have rejected. But you—your bodies will fall in this wilderness. ...For forty years— one year for each of the forty days you explored the land—you will suffer for your sins and know what it is like to have me against you.' I, the LORD, have spoken, and I will surely do these things to this whole wicked community, which has banded together against me. They will meet their end in this wilderness; here they will die." So the men Moses had sent to explore the land...these men respon-

sible for spreading the bad report about the land were struck down and died of a plague before the LORD. Of the men who went to explore the land, only Joshua son of Nun and Caleb son of Jephunneh survived.

Out of the twelve men who spied out the land, only two survived, Caleb and Joshua. In fact, they were the only two adults allowed to enter the Promised Land!

As I was studying this passage, I wrestled greatly as to why things happened the way they did. Why, when twelve men left on the same mission, saw the same thing, went to the same places, and encountered the same events, did ten of them cause a total rebellion and two of them totally believe God? What was the difference?

They all came from the same place—Egypt.

They all lived in the same circumstances.

They all witnessed the same miracles as they went toward the Promised Land.

They all saw the Red Sea split.

Every one of them ate the manna.

They all felt the earth shake when God's presence landed on Mount Sinai. Granted, Joshua had the awesome experience on the mountain with God. But what about Caleb? What made him different? What made him stand up to all his fellow countrymen and defend God?

God's own words about Caleb sum it up best as again we read of God writing a legacy:

But because my servant Caleb has a different spirit and follows me wholeheartedly, I will bring him into the land he went to, and his descendants will inherit it.

Caleb stands in contrast to the other ten spies. They didn't have the same depth of character that Caleb possessed.

Caleb had a personal relationship with God. He was attentive to the things of God. The other men had a surface relationship with God. God met their needs and that was all they really wanted from him. They didn't take the initiative to develop and mature in God. They weren't grateful to God for his blessings. They thought they deserved everything God did for them because they were God's chosen people. Caleb saw it as God being merciful.

God saw Caleb's different spirit and rewarded him for it. He did not die in the wilderness like the people who did not follow God wholeheartedly. While everyone else in his generation wandered in the wilderness and eventually died, Caleb reached his Promised Land.

As we continue through the books of Deuteronomy and Numbers, we find absolutely no mention of Caleb. He is not seen again until the book of Joshua, some forty-five years later. However, through the silent years in the wilderness, Caleb still wholeheartedly followed God and continued developing this legacy.

It may seem like forty years of Caleb's life were wasted in the wilderness. However, nothing with God is ever wasted. God used this time to get all of Egypt out of Caleb.

Caleb needed to remove all the hurt and pain from his time in slavery. He learned new ways of thinking and acting. He needed to become more like God and less like a slave. He learned how to live like a godly man.

Caleb learned how to be a family man. He was taught how to fight for his freedom. He discovered how to overcome the sin in his life. One thing is certain: no matter what happened to Caleb during his time in the wilderness, his faith in God only increased.

At the age of eighty-five, Caleb was finally allowed to enter the Promised Land. If you thought Caleb was a great man of faith when he was young, check out this dude when he was old!

Rather than sitting around reminiscing about the good old days, Caleb's attitude was "What's next?!" Instead of spending his time on a hammock yelling at kids "to get off his sand" or sitting on a bench with the other old-timers and discussing his arthritis or his hip replacement, he fought valiantly against his enemies and completely drove out the inhabitants of the land. How at his age was he able to do it?

The Lord helping me, I will drive them out just as he said.

Then Joshua blessed Caleb son of Jephunneh and gave him Hebron as his inheritance. So Hebron has belonged to Caleb son of Jephunneh the Kenizzite ever since, because he followed the Lord, the God of Israel, wholeheartedly. Joshua 14:12-14

Even at the age of eighty-five, Caleb was still grateful to God for his freedom. He was willing to do whatever God wanted him to do. So he strapped on his sword one more time and destroyed the people who were on God's land. He saw the job that God wanted done, and he did it with everything in him. Caleb started strong and he made sure he finished well! What a tremendous legacy!

Caleb continued his pursuit of following God wholeheartedly by totally defeating his enemies. He completely drove them out, taking sole ownership of the land.

Most of the other Israelites failed to defeat all of their enemies. Those enemies became a source of temptation and sin to them throughout the remainder of their history. Eventually, these enemies led the Israelites into worshiping idols. Because of this sin, God was forced to send them into captivity. However, Caleb was different.

Caleb was so wholeheartedly devoted to God that he completely wiped out his enemies. None of them remained. He conquered all of the land. He was able to live free and at peace for the remainder of his life.

This needs to be our attitude. We need to be grateful to God for all he did for us through Jesus Christ. This gratitude should instill a deep desire in us to never go back to our former way of living. We should long to completely destroy all the enemies that stand in our way.

Our enemy is the sin that is deeply ingrained in us and holds us in bondage or captivity. Because we love God and are grateful to him for setting us free, we must face and destroy anything that remains inside of us that could ever cause us to go back into the bondage of sin.

This will be a lifelong pursuit. The closer we get to God, the more we will see our sinful tendencies. As we see these tendencies and properly destroy them, we will be one step further from our old life of captivity to sin. Like Caleb, we do not have to return to our old life again.

The story of Caleb does not end here. Through God's power, he not only took his Promised Land, but he conquered a part of the Negev. Being a godly man, he gave this land to his daughter. He supplied her with a husband who was worthy of her. He took care of his family and he left his daughter a land that was free from enemies.

Caleb's life should inspire all of us to completely destroy the enemies and sin in our life. If we do this in our lives, our children will have a better understanding of what to be aware of in their lives and what pitfalls to avoid since the generational tendencies are inherited. This is one of my chief goals in life. Let me explain.

I deeply desire to be a man who wholeheartedly serves God. In order to do this, I needed to face the enemies in my life. These enemies are the sins which lived inside me.

One enemy was not respecting women. I come from a long line of men who have little respect for women. They used their wives and daughters as servants, but gave them no love or respect. Overall, women were seen as "less than" men.

My father had absolutely no respect for my mother, her opinions, or the work she did as a wife and mother. He would openly mock my mother. He would put her down to me whenever we were alone. He was emotionally and verbally abusive to my sister. With a lineage like this, I too developed an attitude of disrespect for women.

One day God began to show me how cruelly I treated my mom, sister, and any other women in my life. I realized that rolling my eyes when they give me advice or lashing out at them when they tried to correct me was utter disrespect. I needed to face this enemy and completely drive it out.

That's what I did! I fought this enemy until it was completely destroyed, and now it is not a part of my life.

But let me tell you, it wasn't easy. I spent hours in prayer where the Holy Spirit convicted me of all of my sinful attitudes toward women. Even after I repented, I had to learn new behavioral patterns. I had to learn to talk to women differently, look at women differently, and serve them rather than having them serve me. Like a warrior, I had to attack this enemy of sin with everything I had and choose to overcome this generational sin and become a new man.

Even now, from time to time, I like to do things that will give this old enemy a reminder I'm never going back. When people ask why I volunteer to help out at different women's events, I tell them that I do it to continue dealing a deathblow to my family's old legacy and help make up a little for the awful way men in my family treated women. People who didn't know me then don't believe I was ever like that. That's the power of God helping me defeat an enemy and create a new legacy!

This is an important point for us to learn. We have discussed the fact that we all have enemies of sin living in us. We must never think we have done a good enough job killing these enemies. We must fight these enemies to the death. We cannot let any remain.

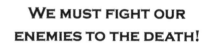

WE MUST FIGHT OUR ENEMIES TO THE DEATH!

The Israelites tolerated a few enemies, and those enemies led them to compromise and sin. Because of this sin, they lost their Promised Land.

We must be ferocious in dealing with these enemies. We must be merciless! We must overcome every last one. This will be a lifelong battle. We must constantly be on our guard to face and destroy any enemies that rear their ugly heads. These sins are ingrained deep inside of us. We must continue the fight until they are all gone.

I don't know what enemies are in your life. It could be lying, stealing, hate, or a hot temper. Maybe you have an enemy in your thought life. Whatever your enemy, I encourage you to face it and destroy it so that you can be wholeheartedly devoted to God.

Freedom is found in defeating your enemies. No one can ever make you go back to your old life of bondage to sin. However, you must never stop fighting your enemies. You must completely annihilate them. This is the best legacy we can leave to our children.

After the account of Caleb giving his daughter an inheritance, we read no more about him in the Bible. He lived in the land God gave him. There isn't even a mention of his death. However, for all of eternity, Caleb will be remembered as a man who was wholeheartedly devoted to God. What an amazing legacy!

A man can do nothing greater with his life than to wholeheartedly love and serve God and to annihilate sin from his life so the next generation is made aware of what needs to be avoided.

This is the mark of a godly man: No matter what happens in life, he is grateful to God and follows him wholeheartedly. This is a man God can use. This is the man I hope you will be inspired to be.

We can all be known as men of wholehearted devotion to God. With wholehearted devotion, we will never go back to our former bondage. We won't desire sin. We will leave the past and press on to what God has for each of us. We will completely drive out our enemies and defeat them. We will allow God to make us the men he wants us to be for our time in history. That is the Caleb legacy, becoming men wholeheartedly devoted to God, men who will NEVER return to our old way of life! We need to start strong, and finish well as we whole-heartedly serve God.

Dear heavenly Father, you know that I have failed at being a man wholeheartedly devoted to you. I need to become a man that is full of gratitude for all you have done for me and a man that will never go back to my old way of life. Forgive me for all of my ingratitude.

Forgive me for all the times I have quit or stopped or failed to continue on with you. Please help me be a strong man who will never shrink back from becoming all that you want me to be.

I want to be a man who wholeheartedly serves you and is dedicated to doing whatever you want whenever you want it. I want my entire body, soul, mind, and spirit to be devoted to doing your will. I want to completely wipe out my enemies so I can live in complete freedom with you. Give me wisdom and strength to do it. In Jesus' name, amen.

LEGACY CHALLENGES

Ask God to reveal to you areas where you are not whole-heartedly following him.

Make a list of any areas that are not completely surrendered to God. Then repent of them and make any necessary changes.

EXTREME LEGACY CHALLENGES

Ask your mentor and/or a trusted friend or family member if they see an area in your life where you are not whole-heartedly devoted to God or have a tendency to go back to your old life. Don't be defensive when they honestly answer you.

GROUP STUDY QUESTIONS

1. What does it mean to be wholeheartedly devoted to God?

2. Are you wholeheartedly devoted to God?

3. What are you grateful to God for freeing you from? How can you express this gratitude?

4. Is there anything holding you back from serving God wholeheartedly?

5. We mentioned Caleb defeated all of his enemies. What are some of the enemies you must defeat? How are you going to defeat them?

6. Can the words God spoke describing Caleb be used to describe you?

6

THE ANANIAS LEGACY

THE NO HIGHWAY OPTION

Recently, I watched a documentary about the man who killed Osama bin Laden. It was a fascinating program as they showed details of how the infamous manhunt came to an end. As I watched the program I couldn't help but remember the events of 9/11, one of the darkest days in American history.

Osama bin Laden was a horrendous terrorist who used any means necessary to accomplish his goals. Throughout history, his name will be remembered as a brutal terrorist—an enemy of all that is good. Until his death, many lived in fear, anticipating what this mastermind of murder was planning next.

Let's take a moment and imagine the following situation. Imagine you had walked into your local grocery store a year after the September 11 tragedies. While paying, you find out that you are the one-millionth customer. You win an all-expense-paid trip to a beach resort in the Middle East. You make plans and leave for your prize-winning vacation.

While on vacation, you turn on the news to hear a scary report. Osama bin Laden has masterminded another attack against American citizens vacationing in the Middle East. He hates the "infidels" as he calls them and vows to destroy all the Americans. The news causes you a bit of fear. Here you are, an American far away from home, and a known killer is vowing to track you down and kill you. This man has no problem kidnapping and beheading people. Right then and there you decide to get on your knees and pray.

You pray for God to protect you and guide you. You pray like David did when he asked God to kill his enemies. All of a sudden your prayer is interrupted by the voice of God.

God speaks to you and says, "I have a job for you. I want you to go to the mountain ranges and enter the third cave you see on your right. Inside you will find Osama bin Laden. I have already told him you were coming. He is waiting for you."

Here you are, a person you know Bin Laden wants to kill. He has killed many like you in the past. You know he has promised to do it in the future. However, you also know the voice of God and what he is telling you to do. My question to you is this: Would you do it?

In our study today, we will be looking at the proper response for a godly man. To learn this lesson, we will meet a man who faced a very similar situation to the one just described. His story is an amazing demonstration of what it takes to develop a legacy as a man who submits to God's will. Let's begin in Acts chapter 9.

AN UNBRIDLED EXTREMIST IS BROKEN

Meanwhile, Saul was still breathing out murderous threats against the Lord's disciples. He went to the high priest and asked him for letters to the synagogues in Damascus, so that if he found any there who belonged to the Way, whether men or women, he might take them as prisoners to Jerusalem.

In this passage we read that Saul, a Pharisee and devout Jew, was angry and full of rage at the Christians. In his eyes, the Christians were destroying the Jewish system of religion. After receiving permission from the high priest, the leading figure in the Jewish religious system, Saul started to take action against the church. He literally became a terrorist declaring a jihad against the Christians.

Saul set out on a trip to Damascus to capture and torture any and all Christians he encountered. He was so obsessed with destroying Christianity that he willingly traveled over a hundred miles on foot to capture them. He was known far and wide for the cruel punishments he would deal out to all the Christians he found. Once in Paul's hands, Christians were forced to either deny Christ or die.

However, God had another plan. On the road to Damascus, Jesus appeared to Saul. The brilliant light of the risen Savior's glory caused Saul to shield his eyes. Jesus spoke to Saul, confronting him about his evil ways and telling Saul that when he persecutes Christians, he is really persecuting God.

This is where the story gets interesting: When Saul asked what he was to do, Jesus commanded him to enter the city where he would be told what to do next. When the light disappeared and Saul opened his eyes, he immediately realized he was blind! The great terrorist was forced to rely on his men to help him into the city to wait for God to reveal what was next for him. He entered the city and took up residence with a man named Judas.

Can you imagine the terror the Christians in Damascus must have felt? They had no idea what had happened to Saul during his travels. All they knew was that the terrorist mastermind had entered their town. At any given moment, they could be sitting in their homes or church when all of a sudden Saul and his thugs could burst through the door and take them all prisoner.

At this point, we are introduced to the man we are going to examine in this chapter. His name is Ananias. He demonstrates the need to submit to God.

AN UNBELIEVABLE REQUEST IS SPOKEN

In Damascus there was a disciple named Ananias. The Lord called to him in a vision, "Ananias!"

"Yes, Lord," he answered.

The Lord told him, "Go to the house of Judas on Straight Street and ask for a man from Tarsus named Saul, for he is praying. In a vision he has seen a man named Ananias come and place his hands on him to restore his sight."

Can you believe what God asked Ananias to do? He wants him to go and meet with the man who came to terrorize Christians!

New flash—Ananias was a Christian! He wasn't just a Christian in name only. Let's look at the description given by Saul of Ananias found in Acts 22:12:

A man named Ananias came to see me. He was a devout observer of the law and highly respected by all the Jews living there.

Saul describes Ananias as a well-known Christian who was devoted to his faith. Saul came to Damascus intent on capturing such a man. Most likely, Ananias was on Saul's hit list. Yet, God didn't want Ananias hiding from Saul. Instead, he wants him to go and seek him out!

The only thing Ananias knew was that Saul had come to his town intent on killing him and other men like him. Now God is ordering him to go and put his own neck into Saul's noose. I don't know about you, but I would have wanted a little bit more information from God. We read this is exactly how Ananias felt.

AN UNDERSTANDABLE REPLY IS GIVEN

"Lord," Ananias answered, "I have heard many reports about this man and all the harm he has done to your holy people in Jerusalem. And he has come here with authority from the chief priests to arrest all who call on your name" (Acts 9:13–14).

Ananias is informing God about Saul as if God had no idea what Saul was going to do to the Christians.

I totally understand Ananias' thought process here. He is basically saying, "Uh, God, this is Saul of Tarsus. He is here to kill your people and that includes me. I know you know how he tortured your people in Jerusalem, and now he has traveled here to get us."

Let's not skip over this too fast or take it too lightly. We know Saul has been converted. Ananias didn't.

God did not reveal this fact to him yet.

He knew Saul as a murderer, not as a blind man being led around by others. However, he also knew he heard God's voice. He knew as a servant of God he had no choice but to do what God commanded. Still, he thought he better make sure it really was God's voice. Let's continue on to find out how God felt about Ananias' words to him.

But the Lord said to Ananias, "Go! This man is my chosen instrument to proclaim my name to the Gentiles and their kings and to the people of Israel. I will show him how much he must suffer for my name.

Don't you love that! I see no anger from God. He doesn't correct Ananias or put him down for seeking further guidance. Instead, we see a God who understands Ananias' human nature and simply reiterates the command. However, this time he gives Ananias the reason for the unbelievable request.

God had a plan for Saul. He was going to use Saul mightily in his kingdom. He was going to let him know what it is like to be a child of

God. Ananias was being given the great blessing of leading the master terrorist into a new life dedicated to following the Christ he had formerly meant to destroy. The final decision, however, was in Ananias' hands.

I don't want to imply that if Ananias refused to do as God commanded, Saul would not be converted. I am sure God would have found another man to do it. However, I believe that before he asked Ananias, God already knew that Ananias would go. He knew that Ananias was a man who would submit to him.

How do we know Ananias was a submissive man? Let me show you two ways.

AN UNWAVERING OBEDIENCE IS ENACTED

The first way Ananias is submissive is seen in the words of Ananias:

*In Damascus there was a disciple named Ananias. The **Lord** called to him in a vision, "Ananias!"*

*"Yes, **Lord**," he answered.*

*The **Lord** told him, "Go to the house of Judas on Straight Street and ask for a man from Tarsus named Saul, for he is praying. In a vision he has seen a man named Ananias come and place his hands on him to restore his sight."*

*"**Lord**," Ananias answered, "I have heard many reports about this man and all the harm he has done to your holy people in Jerusalem. And he has come here with authority from the chief priests to arrest all who call on your name."*

*But the **Lord** said to Ananias, "Go! This man is my chosen instrument to proclaim my name to the Gentiles and their kings and to the people of Israel. I will show him how much he must suffer for my name."*

*Then Ananias went to the house and entered it. Placing his hands on Saul, he said, "Brother Saul, the **Lord**—Jesus, who appeared to you on the road as you were coming here—has sent me...* (emphasis mine).

The Greek word here for *Lord* is *kurios*, which means "pertaining to a master; i.e., one to whom service is due on any grounds."[2] It requires an absolute, unconditional surrender to your master. It describes a willing, conscious submission to God's authority as sovereign ruler of the universe. A truly humble person will give his allegiance to God, obey his commands, and follow his leadership.

Ananias knew that as a Christian he had to do whatever his master ordered. Long ago, he submitted his will to God's will. No longer did he live his life according to what he wanted. Instead, he focused on seeking God and doing God's will. Although it is not mentioned in this passage, Ananias must have proven himself faithful to God in the past by doing what God asked.

Submission to God and his will is the true mark of a godly man. God knew that Ananias was his servant. He knew Ananias would submit to his will and do whatever he asked. Ananias knew God was his Master and had the right to ask him to do whatever he wants whenever he wanted.

> **WHEN A SOLDIER RECEIVES HIS ORDERS, HE ISN'T GIVEN AN OPTION IF HE WANTS TO DO IT OR NOT— HE DOES IT!**

One way to think about this is to examine the military. I love our armed forces. I hold few organizations in higher regard than the military. If I didn't have a physical disability and I hadn't been called into the ministry, I would have loved to be in the military. The military

---

2 W. E. Vine, M. F. Unger, & W. White, *Vine's Complete Expository Dictionary of Old and New Testament Words*, (Nashville: Thomas Nelson, 1996).

is an organization that hinges on ranks and submitting to the man above you. A private can't bad-mouth a sergeant, yet this same sergeant can't bad-mouth his general. When a soldier receives his orders, he isn't given an option whether he wants to do it or not. He does it! You may get to ask a question, but ultimately you do as you're told.

The Christian life is like the military. God is the five-star general. When he gives the orders, you have no choice but to obey. He may allow you to question the order, but in the end you have no choice but to do what God says. Not doing what God asks is disobedience and sin which will cause separation between you and God.

If you are a real follower of God, this is not as hard as it sounds. You will learn to submit your will to God. I am not going to lie to you—at first it will be hard. Our sinful nature doesn't like to be told what to do. After all, we as humans have a natural rebellious streak a mile wide. However, the more we intentionally submit our will and desires to God's will, the easier it gets. Eventually, we reach the point where it will feel unnatural to disobey God.

The concept of submitting my will to God's will has been an ongoing struggle for me. I am a strong-willed man by nature. However, this is not a character trait that is beneficial to my Christian walk. Many times God has forced me to learn to submit to his will. There have been times that God has allowed my body to be injured in order to get me to bend my will to his will. Eventually I learned that his way is the best, and that true happiness is only available when I bend to what he wants.

As I submitted more and more, it became easier. Now I have come to the place where I seek God's will on everything, even small things like what clothing style he wants me to wear. I have learned that God's way is always better than mine, so I want to do what he wants.

Trust me, the more you do God's will, the easier it gets. Do you know why? Because your love for God will grow more and more. As you begin to submit your will to his, you will learn his will is best for you. As a result, you will love him more and want to submit to him more. The reason for submission is just that: it is how you show that you love God and that you want to keep his commandments (John 14:15).

Ananias was a man who was totally submitted to God. He did what God told him to do.

Then Ananias went to the house and entered it. Placing his hands on Saul, he said, "Brother Saul, the Lord—Jesus, who appeared to you on the road as you were coming here—has sent me so that you may see again and be filled with the Holy Spirit.

He submitted his will to God's will and went to see Saul.

Notice he totally submitted. He didn't write Saul a letter. He didn't send a messenger or a singing telegram. He personally left the safety of his home and threw himself into the lion's den by going to see Saul. He did this simply because God told him to do it. Because he loved God, he willingly submitted his will and did what God commanded.

Notice in the above passage the words used by Ananias to Saul. In these words, we see a man who not only submitted to God, but he believed everything God told him. He had absolute confidence in God.

> **AS YOU BEGIN TO SUBMIT YOUR WILL TO GOD'S, YOU WILL LEARN HIS WILL IS BEST FOR YOU, AND YOU WILL WANT TO SUBMIT MORE.**

This is a key in submitting to God. You love God and you know that God has whatever he asks of you under control. Notice what he says.

He said, *"Brother Saul, the Lord—Jesus, who appeared to you on the road as you were coming here—has sent me so that you may see again and be filled with the Holy Spirit."*

Notice he addresses Saul as "Brother Saul." I don't know about you, but if I was walking up to Saul, I don't know if I would have been quite ready to call him *Brother*. However, Ananias had such confidence in God that he went to Saul and immediately recognized Saul was a Christian.

He makes no reference to the evil Saul had committed. He doesn't call him Murderer Saul or Terrorist Saul. God told him Saul was converted, and Ananias totally believed God. His trust in God allowed Ananias to submit his hate and anger for Saul to God, and speak words of love and acceptance to Saul.

Notice that Ananias told Saul that he knew what had happened on the way to Damascus. Making such a claim shows great confidence in what God said. Most people would hesitate to tell this to Saul for fear that they hadn't really heard God. However, Ananias had been commanded by God to tell this to Saul, so he submitted to God and did it.

Ananias' act of submission made a huge impact on Saul. In Acts 22 we read Saul's (then known as Paul's) description of what happened.

Then he [Ananias] said: "The God of our ancestors has chosen you to know his will and to see the Righteous One and to hear words from his mouth. You will be his witness to all people of what you have seen and heard. And now what are you waiting for? Get up, be baptized and wash your sins away, calling on his name."

Ananias boldly proclaimed to this murderer of evangelists that God was going to make him one of the greatest evangelists ever. Then he boldly commands Saul to get up, repent, and be baptized! Only a man who was fully submitted to God would be so obedient. He did exactly what God told him.

This is the mark of a true man. And you know what? He was rewarded by God for his submission.

AN UNDEFINABLE REWARD IS GIVEN

You may be wondering how I know that Ananias received a reward from God. It is a fair question considering that the passage makes no mention of it. Allow me to explain using an example from one of my favorite Christmas movies, *It's a Wonderful Life.*

Most of us have seen this timeless classic during the holidays. However, for those who have never seen it before, allow me to set the stage.

The main character is George Bailey. George was a good, hard-working man with a family. However, George was never satisfied with his life. He always dreamed of traveling the world, being rich and famous. He felt that his life was wasted.

Through a number of different circumstances, George comes to the end of his rope and tries to kill himself. However, an angel appears and stops him and goes on to show George what the world would be like if he had never been born. He sees how his life affected all the friends and family he had.

As George sees what would have happened if he'd have never been born, he is shocked. People were poor and homeless without him. An entire navy ship was destroyed because George's brother Harry, the man who saved them in real life, was dead. Years earlier George had saved Harry's life. By saving Harry's life, George had in essence saved the lives of all the men that were saved by Harry.

Ananias was the same way. Ananias' obedience to God's will led to Saul's conversion. As a result, Saul became the great apostle Paul. He went on at least four missionary journeys, leading many people to Christ. These people led more to Christ, and on and on it goes. Paul wrote thirteen books, just one shy of half of the entire New Testament. How many lives have been converted by reading the words of Paul throughout the years? Because Ananias submitted to God's will and went to visit Saul, he will share in the rewards of all the souls that were saved through Saul's life.

What about you?

Are there things in your life that you feel God leading you to do?

Are you balking at the idea of submitting to God?

I challenge you to begin submitting your will to God's will. Who knows what great accomplishments for God's kingdom are tied up in the one thing God is asking us to do?

Like Ananias, we need to decide whether we are going to submit to God's will or not. It is as basic as that. It involves one step—when God gives the orders, OBEY! This was what characterized the life of Ananias. It is the legacy of submitting your will to God's will. The choice is up to you.

Father, I want to be a man who is completely submitted to you and your will. Please forgive me for every time I have not submitted to you. I understand that I am a man whose natural inclination is to not submit to anyone; however, of my own free will, I choose today to begin to submit my will to yours. Please give me the courage and the strength to do whatever you may ask. Give me an obedient and a submissive heart. As an act of my will, I choose to submit to you and your will. I want to be used by you, and I want to hold nothing back. Thank you Father for loving me. I choose to show my love for you by submitting my will to you. In Jesus' name, amen.

LEGACY CHALLENGES

1. Every morning begin your day by telling God you want to surrender your will to his will today. Ask him to make clear to you what his will is for you. Then do it.

2. Make a list of all the times you can remember not submitting to God's will for you and ask him to forgive you. Be specific.

EXTREME LEGACY CHALLENGES

Is there someone that you have felt led to witness to but for one reason or another been afraid to do so? Submit your will to God and witness to the person—who knows what the end result could be. The person may reject it, or may get saved and go on and lead thousands to Christ. Take the chance and submit to God and leave it in his hands.

GROUP STUDY QUESTIONS

1. Do you feel that it is correct to say Ananias was scared to step out and do what God was telling him to do?

2. Do you agree with the statement that God is our commanding officer and to not follow orders is sin? Why?

3. Do you believe God already knew Ananias would submit before he asked him?

4. How does this statement "submission to God is the way we express love to him" make you feel?

5. Do you agree that Ananias will share in the rewards of Saul's years in ministry?

6. Are there things you feel that God wants you to do that you haven't submitted to him by obeying?

7. Are there things that God doesn't want you to do that you don't want to stop doing?

8. Will you choose to submit to the areas in questions 7 and 8?

7

THE DAVID LEGACY

CONQUERING MANPAIN

How many of you have ever heard the term "manpain"? I first heard this term many years ago while watching an episode of *Home Improvements*; you know, with Tim "The Tool Man" Taylor.

Well, on this particular episode, Tim's wife told him not to lift something heavy, and because he had to prove he was a man, he ignored her and lifted it, pulling his groin in the process. He couldn't tell his wife because he didn't want her to say "I told you so," so he used the code "manpain" when talking to his sons and his friends about the injury.

Now that is physical manpain, a pulled groin. It can also refer to getting hit in the crotch, etc.—the blinding, awful pain you feel when your private area is hurt. That is physical manpain. Today I want to discuss spiritual manpain. We are going to look at what it is, and how it is as devastating to men as a swift kick to the crotch would be.

What is manpain?

It is what I call the deep, emotional pain and wounds inside of us. These wounds are the pain of unmet needs every man has for a man's love and approval. Instead of having these needs met, men suffer emotional wounds because their father or another person emotionally abused them, neglected them, failed them, or abandoned them. This behavior leaves deep, emotional pain inside of us. The sad truth is that most men endure manpain.

We live in a fatherless world. Forty percent of children go to sleep at night in a different home from their fathers. Four out of ten kids! These kids go through life without a father's love, influence, advice, and guidance. However, these forty percent are not the only ones in danger of manpain.

Many kids have fathers in their home at bedtime, but have no dad present in their lives. These fathers put careers and success ahead of their children. Meetings and schedules take precedence over family life. These kids grow up having no idea what it means to have a dad. The irony of the situation is that many of their fathers are so engrossed in their careers and making something of themselves because *they themselves* suffer from manpain. They need to prove to themselves, as well as to their own fathers, that they are real men. However, they don't realize that trying to ease their manpain is resulting in the same pain being developed in their sons.

Many men develop manpain from the physical and emotional abuse they receive growing up. Some have deep emotional pain from growing up with a father who beat them every day of their lives. Others suffer manpain not because of a physical beating, but because of the cruel, abusive words constantly spoken to them. Trust me, I know from firsthand experience, being publicly humiliated by a screaming father is just as scarring as a thumping from him. Both leave scars. Manpain.

Manpain is all around us. Men go through life trying to hide this deep pain inside their hearts. Men try to ease the pain by using drugs, alcohol, sex, success, and a host of other vices, but this only causes the pain to increase. However, it doesn't go away.

Manpain has men all over the world trapped in its painful clutches. They live their lives struggling to break free, only to find they are passing their pain on to their children.

This cycle of pain must stop. The pattern must be broken. We need to stand up as men of God and say enough is enough. We must face the pain, recognize the damage, work on healing it, and begin moving forward as healthy, vibrant men.

This is the only way we can realize true joy and happiness. Only then can our marriages thrive and blossom.

Overcoming manpain allows us to break the bonds of sexual bondage in our lives. It helps us be able to experience true success in life. It enables us to develop a new legacy.

Breaking the grips that manpain has on us is the only chance we have of breaking the generational patterns that have dominated our families for way too long. It is the only way to achieve peace in our lives.

Facing the manpain allows us to break free of the pain. We can begin to forgive our fathers and other men who have hurt us, realizing that they too suffer from manpain. Then, we can move forward, free of hatred and bitterness. We will be free to follow and serve God in a more intimate way than ever. It will hurt to address the pain, but once dealt with, we will be free to experience life like God intended.

How do we do it? In the pages of the Bible, we find the story of David—his story greatly helped me when I was forced to face my manpain. If ever there was a man who should have felt manpain, it was David.

David is one of the most popular men in the Bible. He is mainly remembered for killing Goliath and being Israel's greatest king. Many know him as "a man after God's own heart." What a legacy! I don't know about you, but I would love for that to be my legacy. David was one of the godliest men to ever live. He was a brave warrior, a masterful politician, a gentle poet, and an exemplary worshipper of God. However, he also suffered from manpain.

The first time we read of David is in 1 Samuel 16 (NKJV).

Now the LORD said to Samuel, "How long will you mourn for Saul, seeing I have rejected him from reigning over Israel? Fill your horn with oil, and go; I am sending you to Jesse the Bethlehemite. For I have provided Myself a king among his sons."

Saul, the current king of Israel, had lost God's blessing on his life and reign. Israel needed a new king. Samuel, the prophet of the nation of Israel, was sent by God to David's family to find the man God wanted. As we read on, we see that Jesse gathered all of his sons for Samuel to interview—all, that is, except David.

So it was, when they came, that he [Samuel] looked at Eliab [Jesse's oldest son] and said, "Surely the LORD's anointed is before Him!"

But the LORD said to Samuel, "Do not look at his appearance or at his physical stature, because I have refused him. For the LORD does not see as man sees; for man looks at the outward appearance, but the LORD looks at the heart." So Jesse called Abinadab, and made him pass before Samuel. And he said, "Neither has the LORD chosen this one." Then Jesse made Shammah pass by. And he said, "Neither has the LORD chosen this one." Thus Jesse made seven of his sons pass before Samuel. And Samuel said to Jesse, "The LORD has not chosen these." And Samuel said to Jesse, "Are all the young men here?" Then he said, "There remains yet the youngest, and there he is, keeping the sheep."

Do you believe it? Jesse thought so little of David that he didn't even invite him to the family reunion. He felt there was no way God would ever want David. All he felt David was good for was being a shepherd.

In today's day and age, being a shepherd is not a bad thing. However in David's time, there was no worse profession for a Jew. Shepherds were ceremonially unclean. They were not allowed to go into the temple area to worship. They were unaccepted. They were nobodies. They could not be called as witnesses in court, for somebody had written that no one could believe the testimony of a shepherd. They were despised. They were looked down upon and often hated. The Jewish Talmud says of them, "Give no help to a heathen or to a shepherd."

Shepherds were considered the least of all men. Jesse thought David was capable of no better. If ever a man should well up at the mention of his father, it was David.

Eventually Samuel found out that David was excluded from the festivities. He demanded David be brought out of the fields to stand before him. He immediately recognized that David was the one God wanted as king. He anointed David and blessed him. However, this did little to change David's relationship with his father. We see this as we move forward through the book of 1 Samuel.

But the Spirit of the LORD departed from Saul, and a distressing spirit from the LORD troubled him.

We read here that the king of Israel was suffering from a tormenting spirit which was allowed by God. In order to relieve the torment, his servant had a good idea. He suggests having someone come in and play some music for Saul, hoping it would soothe Saul's foul mood. As a result, someone suggested David be summoned for the job.

Then one of the servants answered and said, "Look, I have seen a son of Jesse the Bethlehemite, who is skillful in playing, a mighty man of valor, a man of war, prudent in speech, and a handsome person; and the LORD is with him."

David was singled out as the gifted man to come and help relieve the king. Apparently, David's accomplishments as a musician and man of character were not unnoticed by the people in the king's court. However, they were ignored by the man that David needed support from the most...his father.

Therefore Saul sent messengers to Jesse, and said, "Send me your son David, who is with the sheep."

The fact that David had been anointed by Samuel apparently had no effect on the way his father viewed him, because we read here that Jesse sent David back out into the fields with the sheep. David struggled to gain his father's approval. He had a horrendous relationship with his dad. In Psalms 27:10 David sums up his relationship with his father.

When my father and my mother forsake me, Then the LORD will take care of me.

David felt he was abandoned and forsaken by his father! He longed for male acceptance. After all, you can only be declared a man by another man. Yet David never seemed to get this approval from Jesse. Eventually, we read that he began to look elsewhere to have this need met.

Like many of us, David tried to ease his manpain by seeking a male mentor. However, he couldn't seem to find one. He certainly didn't receive love and acceptance from his older brothers. We read this as we see David's father continuing to treat David like a servant instead of a son. I Samuel 17:12.

Now David was the son of that Ephrathite of Bethlehem Judah, whose name was Jesse, and who had eight sons. ...The three oldest sons of Jesse had gone to follow Saul to the battle. ...David was the youngest. And the three oldest followed Saul. But David occasionally went and returned from Saul to feed his father's sheep at Bethlehem.

...Then Jesse said to his son David, "Take now for your brothers an ephah of this dried grain and these ten loaves, and run to your brothers at the camp. And carry these ten cheeses to the captain of their thousand, and see how your brothers fare, and bring back news of them.

David was sent by his father to check on his brothers. Normally a younger brother longs to receive the acceptance of his older brothers, especially when this need isn't met by his father. However, the brothers didn't exactly give David a warm welcome.

Now Eliab his oldest brother heard when he spoke to the men; and Eliab's anger was aroused against David, and he said, "Why did you come down here? And with whom have you left those few sheep in the wilderness? I know your pride and the insolence of your heart, for you have come down to see the battle."

Once again David receives rejection from the older men in his life. Like his father, Eliab had a low opinion of David. He let everyone there know that David was just a dirty little shepherd. He ridiculed David's job, his character, and his behavior. He put David in his place and let him know he was no good. He was just a dirty, unclean shepherd who nobody wanted around.

David's pursuit of a man's acceptance once again took a blow. However, he didn't stop there—he kept looking. As we read on, it appears he may have finally found it.

After enduring the public ridicule of his older brother, God used David to defeat Goliath. Instantly, David became a national hero. As a result, he entered into life in King Saul's court. While there, he met Jonathan.

Then, as David returned from the slaughter of the Philistine, Abner took him and brought him before Saul with the head of the

Philistine in his hand. And Saul said to him, "Whose son are you, young man?"

So David answered, "I am the son of your servant Jesse the Bethlehemite."

Now when he had finished speaking to Saul, the soul of Jonathan was knit to the soul of David, and Jonathan loved him as his own soul. Saul took him that day, and would not let him go home to his father's house anymore. Then Jonathan and David made a covenant, because he loved him as his own soul. And Jonathan took off the robe that was on him and gave it to David, with his armor, even to his sword and his bow and his belt.

So David went out wherever Saul sent him, and behaved wisely. And Saul set him over the men of war, and he was accepted in the sight of all the people and also in the sight of Saul's servants.

David found a home with Saul and his family. They trusted him, honored him, loved him, and treated him with dignity and respect. In Jonathan, David found the acceptance he had long been searching for. Jonathan was quite a bit older than David. He became a mentor and friend to David. For the first time in years, David felt relief from his manpain. However, this didn't last.

Now it had happened as they were coming home, when David was returning from the slaughter of the Philistine, that the women had come out of all the cities of Israel, singing and dancing, to meet King Saul, with tambourines, with joy, and with musical instruments. So the women sang as they danced, and said:

"Saul has slain his thousands,

And David his ten thousands."

Then Saul was very angry, and the saying displeased him; and he said, "They have ascribed to David ten thousands, and to me they have ascribed only thousands. Now what more can he have but the kingdom?" So Saul eyed David from that day forward.

David's success caused the mentally disturbed Saul to be jealous. Saul wasn't about to let a dirty shepherd take his place. His heart drastically changed toward David. Instead of honoring him, he tried to kill him.

Twice Saul tried to murder David, and twice he escaped. After the second time, David was forced to flee permanently. As a result, he lost contact with his close friend and mentor, Jonathan.

David ended up alone, on the run, and hurting deep inside from the abuse he endured from his father and other men. However, the abuse didn't end. While David ran from Saul, he managed to gather a group of younger men around him who were in the same situation as him. David trained these men into a good army. David found loyal and faithful men who would give their lives for him. It appeared he had finally found male acceptance and camaraderie. However, it wasn't the end of the manpain in David's life.

Although David found companionship among these men, he failed to fully overcome the affects of manpain. One day, the issue reasserted itself.

As David and his men hid in caves to avoid Saul, they came across some shepherds who worked for a man named Nabal. David and his men became bodyguards for the shepherds and their flocks. In return, David expected to be given some of the food that would come when Nabal butchered his sheep. David sent men to Nabal asking for a share of the celebration since they had protected the flock and Nabal's men (1 Samuel 25 NKJV).

David was sure Nabal would do it. He was wrong.

Then Nabal answered David's servants, and said, "Who is David, and who is the son of Jesse? There are many servants nowadays who break away each one from his master. Shall I then take my bread and my water and my meat that I have killed for my shearers, and give it to men when I do not know where they are from?"

Once again, David is ridiculed. However, this time is different. As we look at the rest of this passage, we will see why it is so important to deal with our manpain. Let's look at David's reaction to see what I mean.

So David's young men turned on their heels and went back; and they came and told him all these words. Then David said to his men, "Every man gird on his sword." So every man girded on his sword, and David also girded on his sword. And about four hundred men went with David.

> **WE CAN ONLY BURY OUR PAIN FOR SO LONG. IT WILL EVENTUALLY COME OUT. LEFT UNDEALT WITH, WE WILL BEGIN TO ACT JUST LIKE THE MAN WHO CAUSED OUR MANPAIN.**

David had had enough! He had been harassed and ridiculed for the last time! Nabal ridiculed David as a nobody who was no good. He put down his reputation, his lineage, and his name. Nabal would pay for his words with his life. I believe Nabal was about to pay for the abuse and neglect that David had received from his father, brothers, and Saul.

David had reached his breaking point. He had buried his pain for too long. Eventually, he popped. If we refuse to deal with the pain in our hearts, we will too.

We, as human beings, can only bury our pain for so long. It will eventually come out. Left undealt with, we will begin to act just like the man who caused our manpain. Our manpain will expose itself.

It may come out in a violent outburst like the one David was about to have. It may reveal itself in a failed marriage because the pain in our heart keeps us from fully giving our heart to our wife. It could be exposed through a heart attack, Alzheimer's, a stroke, or some other form of physical problem because we held the pain inside for too long. We may even see it when our kids end up in trouble because we weren't around enough as we prove our manhood by being a workaholic. For each person the result will be different, but the devastation will come in some way if we refuse to deal with our manpain. Luckily for David, he was forced to face it and overcome. We see this as David begins his trek to separate Nabal's head from his shoulders.

As we return to the passage, we find that Nabal's wife, Abigail, is told about Nabal's words to David and David's angry response. Abigail quickly jumped into action and went to David. As we return to the passage, we see that David gets his eyes off his manpain and onto the proper things.

> *Now when Abigail saw David, she dismounted quickly from the donkey, fell on her face before David, and bowed down to the ground. So she fell at his feet and said: "On me, my lord, on me let this iniquity be! And please let your maidservant speak in your ears, and hear the words of your maidservant. Please, let not my lord regard this scoundrel Nabal. For as his name is, so is he: Nabal is his name, and folly is with him!*

DAVID WAS FOCUSED ON GETTING LOVE, RESPECT, AND ACCEPTANCE FROM OTHER MEN. ABIGAIL REFOCUSED DAVID'S ATTENTION TO THE FACT THAT DAVID ALREADY HAD THIS ACCEPTANCE FROM GOD.

Abigail quickly tries to calm David's anger. She starts by telling him that Nabal isn't worth David betraying his own good name. She knew Nabal was wrong and begged David for forgiveness and mercy.

As we continue on, we see Abigail redirect David from his anger. As she does, David is forced to once and for all face his manpain.

> *For the LORD will certainly make for my lord an enduring house, because my lord fights the battles of the LORD, and evil is not found in you throughout your days. Yet a man has risen to pursue you and seek your life, but the life of my lord shall be bound in the bundle of the living with the LORD your God; and the lives of your enemies He shall sling out, as from the pocket of a sling. And it shall come to pass, when the LORD has done for my lord according to all the good that He has spoken concerning you, and has appointed you ruler over Israel, that this will be no grief to you, nor offense of heart to my lord, either that you have shed blood without cause, or that my lord has avenged himself.*

David made the mistake that we all make in dealing with his manpain—he focused on getting love, respect, and acceptance from other men. Abigail refocused David's attention to the fact that David *already* had this acceptance from God.

It didn't matter what her husband thought of David. It didn't matter if David's father liked him. It didn't even matter that Saul was trying to kill him.

God loved David. He chose David to be his son. No one could harm him. No one could belittle him. No man could touch David. God loved him, accepted him, and wanted him as his own. All of David's needs could be met by God and God alone. The same is true for us.

No human man, not our fathers, our friends, our mentors, or even our pastors can ever fully meet our needs. They can never take away the pain and rejection we feel inside. They will never give us everything we want and need. Only God can do this.

Humans are sinful beings. They all fail. Even the "Father of the Year" can't meet your needs. Only God can do this.

The good news is he is ready and willing. He adopted you. He hand-chose you. He longs for you to run into his arms and call him Daddy. He did it for David, and he will do it for us.

David learned to turn to God for everything. David started out life as a young man with extreme manpain. He was rejected, despised, abused, belittled, neglected, and unwanted. For most of his life, he reached out to men for companionship, guidance, acceptance, and love. Most of these men gave him nothing but a swift kick in the pants. There is no better example of a manpain–damaged guy than David. However, he didn't stay that way. He faced his manpain and turned out to be one of the most godly men to ever live. If he could do it, so can we.

You may be asking, "Jamie, how do you know David overcame his manpain?"

To find the answer to this question, we need only to turn to 2 Samuel 16 (NKJV). This chapter takes place when David is forced to flee for his life from his son, Absalom, who was trying to steal his kingdom. As David and his most trusted allies flee the city, they come across a man named Shimei.

Now when King David came to Bahurim, there was a man from the family of the house of Saul, whose name was Shimei the son of Gera, coming from there. He came out, cursing continuously as he came. And he threw stones at David and at all the servants of King David. And all the people and all the mighty men were on his right hand and on his left. Also Shimei said thus when he cursed: "Come out! Come out! You bloodthirsty man, you rogue! The LORD has brought upon you all the blood of the house of Saul, in whose place you have reigned; and the LORD has delivered the kingdom into the hand of Absalom your son. So now you are caught in your own evil, because you are a bloodthirsty man!"

How's that for an insult on David's manhood! It's equal to the treatment David received from his dad, and worse than what Nabal threw at him. If these words weren't insulting enough, look at what Shimei does in verse 13.

And as David and his men went along the road, Shimei went along the hillside opposite him and cursed as he went, threw stones at him and kicked up dust.

He actually threw rocks at David! We would expect David to want this man's head. His men certainly did.

Then Abishai the son of Zeruiah said to the king, "Why should this dead dog curse my lord the king? Please, let me go over and take off his head!"

Abishai is ready to bring the boom! Abishai was one of David's most trusted men. He was there with David throughout David's time on the run from Saul. He knew David, and he wanted to defend him. Shimei was as good as dead.

Wrong. David had dealt with his manpain. I can prove it in verses 11 and 12.

And David said to Abishai and all his servants, "See how my son who came from my own body seeks my life. How much more now may this Benjamite? Let him alone, and let him curse; for so the LORD has ordered him. It may be that the LORD will look on my affliction, and that the LORD will repay me with good for his cursing this day.

David didn't react in anger. He now knew who he was in God. He got his esteem and worth from his relationship with God. He knew it didn't matter what Shimei thought of him. He believed God loved him and would vindicate him, just like Abigail had taught him many years earlier.

David overcame his manpain. We need to learn from his example.

David did what we all need to do. He faced his manpain. He went before God and sought his healing power. He faced the memories of how his father treated him and how it affected him. He let God expose the pain and set him free of it so he could move forward free of the hurt. He expressed openly and honestly the pain he felt inside his heart. He didn't close God out, fearful of another man rejecting him. Instead, he ran right into God's arms. He let God love him.

David became vulnerable with God. He held nothing back. If he felt angry, he told God. If he felt alone, he turned to God for comfort. When he felt falsely accused, he laid out his case before God and waited for God to vindicate him.

David didn't run from God, fearful of being vulnerable. He got his self-worth from God. He spent time alone with God. David got to know God intimately. God knew David's heart and how to get through the damaged heart, the inability to trust anyone, and the pain in his soul. He can do the same for you.

How do I know this? God did it in my life.

As I've said before, I grew up idolizing my dad. I loved spending time with him. When he came home from work, I would run to him as he walked through the door. All I ever wanted was to be with my dad. Unfortunately, he didn't feel the same.

To be fair, my dad had a lot of manpain of his own in his life. Because of issues in his past, he shut down his emotions and never allowed anyone into his life. As an adult who has spent years dealing with my manpain, I have come to understand this; however, as I child, I had no clue why my dad treated me the way he did.

I was subjected to great amounts of emotional and mental abuse growing up. This abuse left me fearful of my dad and all men, yet inside I longed for his love and acceptance. It took me years to understand that my dad is incapable of having truly healthy relationships, and I had to learn to love him in spite of his inability to give me the approval I desired.

Like David, I looked elsewhere for these needs to be met. In college, I found my Jonathan in a godly professor. He accepted me, encouraged me, and built me up. For a short time my manpain was eased. However, it didn't go away. Like David, life separated me from this godly man. It was after this I had to once and for all face my manpain and deal with it.

God had me return home after college to live with my parents. All of a sudden, the old issues of pain and anger inside of me toward my father resurfaced. God began to make me sort through all the abuse and pain in my heart. It wasn't easy.

> THE BEST WAY TO OVERCOME MANPAIN IS BY DEVELOPING A RELATIONSHIP WITH GOD. ALL RELATIONSHIPS REQUIRE COMMUNICATION. PRAYER IS THE ARTERY THAT CONNECTS YOU TO THE HEART OF GOD.

The pivotal night came when my father made me so angry that I put my fist through a wooden door. I was instantly heartbroken that I was capable of such a violent outburst. I knew I needed help.

I eventually began working through the painful memories of the extreme emotional, mental, and slight physical abuse that I endured throughout life. After many hours in prayer, I began to realize it didn't matter what my dad or any other man thought of me. God loved me. He wanted me. He chose me before I was born to be his child. I could find the love and acceptance I desperately wanted when I ran into his arms. God set me free from my manpain just like he set David free from his. He will do the same for you.

The best way to overcome manpain is by developing a relationship with God. All relationships require communication. Prayer is the artery that connects you to the heart of God. Be honest with God in your prayers. Tell him that you never felt loved in your life and you want to experience his love. Allow him to show you the garbage in your past that is hindering you from accepting his love. This is a prayer that God will answer. This prayer lines up perfectly with his will because he longs for us to be free to experience his love.

God really does love you. No matter how your own father has treated you or what he did to you, it is in no way a representation of how God feels about you. He loves you at all times. Even when you sin, he loves you.

God is the only one that can fill the void inside your heart. Only he can remove the manpain. He can take your broken, wounded, and battered heart and fill it with love. Then, like David, you will be free to become a man after God's own heart. All he requires is that you face the pain, bring it to him, and allow him to love and heal you. I know firsthand he will do it.

As we come to a close I want to share something with you that I wrote during the time I began to experience freedom from my man-pain. It is called, "Who Am I."

> I am a man like so many of you. I am the son of my father. We all have a father. Some men's fathers are men to model, full of character and dignity. Some men's fathers are deserters, abandoning a son who needs them. Then there are fathers who don't desert their sons physically, but are nowhere to be found mentally or emotionally. No matter what type of father you have, you are still someone's son, just like me.

> I am a man, searching for love and acceptance. I am a man looking for his father's pride and approval, just like you. I am a man, who, if he doesn't receive it from his father, looks to someone else. Some look to a girlfriend, some to

sex, some to drugs and alcohol, some to a mentor, or some to an admired friend. I am a man like you who has looked elsewhere for a father's love, only to come back disappointed, empty, and alone.

I am a man, who, in extreme desperation, turned to the Holy Bible. I learned I am a man who is loved by God. I have an adopted Father who loves me and wants me. Unlike the other men I turned to in life, this Father fills all of my needs. He fills me and makes me complete.

I am a man with an advocate. I am a man with a protector. I receive unconditional love. I have a Father who loves me enough to discipline me. My Father keeps every one of his promises. He laughs with me through the good times and carries me through the bad. Who am I? I am a child of God! He is my Father, and I am his boy.

I am a man who has found complete satisfaction. I accept myself, not for who I am, but what God can make me to be. My search is over, my needs are fulfilled as I daily cry out, "Abba, Father."

You are a man just like me. It doesn't matter who your dad is or what you have done. Complete love, forgiveness, and acceptance can be yours when you cry out to God. You are a man like me. You are God's boy.

Dear heavenly Father, I am tired of letting my life and my emotions be consumed and controlled by manpain. I ask you to forgive me for allowing manpain to have such a control on my life. Father, please break the grip manpain has on me.

Father, I know that only you can fill the holes inside of me. No other man can fill it. Drugs can't fill it. Women can't fill it. Only you can meet every one of my needs. Work inside of me and help me to allow you to heal my manpain. In Jesus' name, amen.

LEGACY CHALLENGES

In order to deal with your manpain, you need to first face that it is there. Spend time with God in prayer asking him to show you:

1. Who caused your manpain?
2. How manpain affects your daily life.
3. How manpain affects your relationships.
4. How manpain affects your spiritual life.
5. What you do to ease your manpain.

Then ask God to heal your manpain. Ask God to fill the needs in your life. Ask him to be the one that meets the needs for love and acceptance so you can break free of manpain and live as a victorious son of God.

EXTREME LEGACY CHALLENGES

In this chapter, I discussed how I had to come to the place of showing mercy to my father and realize he too suffered from manpain. Honestly look at the life and background of the people who caused your manpain.

What in their past caused them to act the way they did? You need to do this, not to excuse their behavior, but to help you overcome. You need to have mercy on them and look at them through the eyes of an adult, not the eyes of a hurting child in need of love and acceptance.

After you do this, share what you discovered with a trusted friend or mentor.

GROUP STUDY QUESTIONS

1. How has manpain affected your life?

2. Who caused your manpain?

3. We mentioned some men turn to sex, drugs, alcohol, success, etc., to fill their manpain. What do you turn to ease your manpain?

4. Did you have a Jonathan in your life? Was he able to fill your needs?

5. We said David reached his breaking point with Nabal and he snapped, ready to give Nabal his years of pent-up manpain. Have you experienced a breaking point? What was it? How did you react?

6. We discussed how David was vulnerable with God and expressed all his thoughts with God, both the good and the bad. Do you do this with God? If the answer is no, why not?

7. How does prayer help us overcome manpain?

8. How can we as a group help you face your manpain?

8

THE JOSEPH LEGACY

STAYING PURE IN
AN IMPURE WORLD

Growing up in the mountainous area of Pennsylvania, I am accustomed to seeing many of God's beautiful creatures. Quite often they are roaming around our yard. From the safety of our house, we have seen deer, squirrels, rabbits, possums, bears, and foxes. Each animal has distinct beauty and attributes. However, there is one creature whose beauty always amazes me whenever I see it roaming our property.

This particular animal is stunning to look at. Its fur is so luscious and beautiful. It shines so elegantly. It is the deepest color black you could ever see. It walks proud and upright. Its beauty and grace is unmatched in the wooded area around my house. What is this stunning creature? It is a skunk.

Does that answer surprise you? Most people do not look at skunks as things of beauty. They are more known for the horrible stench they spray. Skunks are not revered or admired, they are feared. When you get sprayed by a skunk, it affects your life for days, sometimes weeks. The stench lingers a LONG time. If you hit a skunk with a car, it will stink for ages. Sometimes it can even get into the fabric and permanently ruin it.

When I was in college, we had a skunk take up residence underneath our dorm. It popped out from time to time. I remember once some friends and I came back from a McDonald's run and saw the skunk sitting right on the front step of the dorm. We were so worried that someone would innocently open the door and get an unwelcome greeting right in the kisser.

Every year our school had a big banquet at the end of the year. It was THE event of the year. It was always in the spring, when the weather turned nice. This particular spring was unusually warm, so most of us had our dorm windows open. That's when our friendly neighborhood skunk decided to go for a stroll around the building. One of the freshmen saw it, got scared, and decided to chase the skunk away by throwing stuff at him. You can imagine what happened next!

The skunk let 'er rip! The smell infiltrated every window. Our clothes stank, we stank, it was awful. Then it hit everyone that our good clothes, which were washed, ironed, and ready for the banquet, now smelled like skunk!

Finally, one of my friends had had enough of this skunk. Knowing that once a skunk sprays it can't do it again for a few hours, he and another guy decided it was time to kill the skunk once and for all. They covered themselves in garbage bags from head to toe, grabbed some shovels, and set out to eliminate the enemy. They came back an hour later. They had tracked down, killed, and buried the skunk.

So why am I telling you all this about skunks? Because I want you to see an interesting fact about men. Even though a skunk is a beautiful creature, most of us have enough common sense not to mess with it. They are smelly, destructive, and have the potential to cause great damage to us and our lives. If men are smart enough to figure this out, then why are so many men unable to avoid pornography?

"Whoa, Jamie, where did that come from?" Well, think about it. Men look at the beautiful women in pornography, gaze at their seductiveness, and lust after their sexual appeal. They fantasize about these beautiful women. Yet they fail to realize that pornography is way more destructive than a skunk could ever be.

Pornography will ruin a man's life. It is THE most addictive thing in the world. When men see a pornographic image, it releases a special chemical in our brain which causes the memory to be etched in our minds. That is one reason it is so hard to break free of pornography.

Pornography is one of the leading causes of divorce. Many marriages are destroyed by it. Pornography causes men to look at woman as objects. They lose sight of the humanness of women, often leading to abuse. Porn causes men to lose touch with reality.

They live in a fantasy world where the women never have needs or problems in life. The images are not real women. They never grow old and their looks never change. When they do, there is always another girl to replace them. Then men date or are married to real women with emotional and physical problems. These men have unrealistic expectations for the women in their lives, and when the expectations aren't met, these men eventually end up divorced.

Pornography opens the door to marital infidelity. Men who would never cheat on their wives begin to find themselves attracted to the woman at work or the clerk at the store. Before you know it, marriages are destroyed and lives are ruined.

Pornography is such a dangerous trap, way more dangerous than a skunk could ever be. But many men take more precautions with a skunk then they ever do with their TV or Internet. In the words of the apostle James, *"Brothers, this should not be so."*

Every man has the choice of how to deal with pornography in their lives. You can either deal with it like the freshman dealt with the skunk and just throw a bottle at it and not take it seriously, or you can do what my friend did and take strong action and kill it in your life.

We need to be men who begin to take pornography seriously. We need to learn how to resist its temptations and be victorious. Thankfully, the Bible gives us the example of a man who had a tremendous legacy of standing pure sexually in the midst of the battle. I personally learned a lot from Joseph during my battle of overcoming watching pornography. While I never actually followed through with my desires or lost my virginity, I was stuck in the cycle of watching porn again and again. I wanted to quit, but I ended up failing over and over. God used Joseph's story to help me gain victory. That's why I wanted to add this man's legacy to this book, to help other men trapped in the filth of porn break free and be victorious.

From Joseph's example, we will learn how to refuse to sin sexually, to resist sexual opportunities, and to run from sexual temptations. Guys, we can all develop a legacy of sexual purity.

We live in a culture where sensuality and perversion dominate our lives. Sex is used to manipulate, control, and sell. We are bombarded daily with images through the TV, Internet, magazines, and even newspaper ads. Hollywood is constantly bombarding us with their images of a real man.

Our society views a real man as a ladies' man—someone who has sex with a different girl each night. They say a man is a fool to marry young because there are so many beautiful women to have sex with before tying yourself down to one woman. The more women he sleeps with, the better a man he is.

This is one of Satan's biggest lies, used to destroy the lives of men. I have learned and I firmly believe it is possible to live a pure and holy life in the area of sex. God showed me ways to do it, and you can do it, too.

Joseph was one of Jacob's twelve sons. Joseph was "the chosen son." He was his dad's favorite, which caused his brothers to hate him. Eventually their hate took over and they sold him into slavery. We are going to pick up Joseph's story while he is a slave in Egypt. In Genesis 39, you will see that he became a success in Egypt.

Now Joseph had been taken down to Egypt. Potiphar, an Egyptian who was one of Pharaoh's officials, the captain of the guard, bought him from the Ishmaelites who had taken him there.

Joseph was sold as a slave to Potiphar, who was the chief of the executioners, an elite force in Pharaoh's army. This was one tough dude Joseph now served! Think of men like Vin Diesel or "The Rock," Dwayne Johnson. Joseph had to grow up fast to survive in this man's household.

The LORD was with Joseph so that he prospered, and he lived in the house of his Egyptian master. When his master saw that the LORD was with him and that the LORD gave him success in everything he did, Joseph found favor in his eyes and became his attendant.

The secret to Joseph's success in Egypt was that he learned to rely on the Lord. As a result, the Lord rewarded him by giving him favor and blessing in all he did. However, this was not the end of the rewards for Joseph:

Potiphar put him in charge of his household, and he entrusted to his care everything he owned. From the time he put him in charge of his household and of all that he owned, the LORD blessed the household of the Egyptian because of Joseph. The blessing of the LORD was on everything Potiphar had, both in the house and in the field. So Potiphar left everything he had in Joseph's care; with Joseph in charge, he did not concern himself with anything except the food he ate.

Joseph, the man who started out as a beloved son, despised brother, and now a slave became the most powerful man in the household of one of Egypt's most powerful leaders. Notice it says he controlled everything except what Potiphar ate. Joseph was never questioned. He had free reign. What could possibly go wrong?

Now Joseph was well-built and handsome.

Apparently Joseph was *the man*, the Brad Pitt or Chris Hemsworth of Egypt. Joseph relied on God, overcame adversity, and become a huge success in Egypt. Who cares what he looks like? While this statement seems out of place, it is the transition into the next part of Joseph's life. Let's continue looking at the Scripture.

And after a while his master's wife took notice of Joseph and said, "Come to bed with me!"

That is what is known as the direct approach! She saw that Joseph was good-looking and she wanted to sleep with him.

Now, let's take a reality check here, guys. Most of us will go through life and never have anything like this happen to us. However, we will all face situations that will open us up to sexual temptation. It could be something we see on TV, or be as innocent as a woman bending over to pick up something. These things can open the sight-driven male mind to be tempted to commit sexual sin. It is our job to be a godly man and not allow our integrity to be challenged. As we continue through this chapter, I want to share with you three ways we can overcome sexual temptation.

WE MUST DECIDE TO REFUSE TO SIN

The first way that Joseph overcame sexual sin was by refusing to give in to his desires and commit a sexual sin.

But he refused. "With me in charge," he told her, "my master does not concern himself with anything in the house; everything he owns he has entrusted to my care. No one is greater in this house than I am. My master has withheld nothing from me except you, because you are his wife. How then could I do such a wicked thing and sin against God?"

Faced with an extreme temptation, he stood firm and refused to sin sexually. Understand how significant this is.

Joseph was a slave who had free reign over Potiphar's entire household. Potiphar had complete trust in Joseph. He had achieved great success. He was at the pinnacle of his career. Who knows what opportunities could have been afforded him if he had just slept with her?

Still, Joseph chose not to do it.

Why? If we look back at the passage, we see three reasons why Joseph did not consider her advances.

> **JOSEPH KNEW HIS LIFE WAS AN OPEN BOOK BEFORE GOD, AND HE COULD NOT COMMIT SUCH BLATANT SIN AGAINST HIS GOD!**

The first reason Joseph refused her is because he didn't want to betray Potiphar's trust. If Joseph had an affair with Potiphar's wife, he would totally destroy his good reputation. He respected Potiphar, he respected the institution of marriage, and he wouldn't allow her advances to destroy these relationships.

I wonder how many men stop to think how many lives they ruin, hurt, and destroy when they have sex outside of marriage? It causes life-changing damage to the spouse and children involved. It hurts co-workers, friends, and churches. It is not just a private act. It kills relationships and destroys reputations. Joseph was not going to have any of that in his life. He would not betray Potiphar, and more importantly, he would not betray himself.

The second reason why Joseph would not give in to her advances is he refused to sin against his God. This is the biggest reason, even more important than Potiphar's opinion of him.

How then could I do such a wicked thing and sin against God?

Joseph knew something that Mrs. Potiphar didn't know—his life was an open book before God, and he could not commit such blatant sin against his God. He was a normal young man with the same desires we all face, but Joseph's God was more real to him than anything or anyone else on earth. Instead, he made the choice to walk away.

Men, we have a responsibility before God to stay sexually pure. While sexual sin affects a lot of people, it is really a sin against God. David, after being caught having an affair with Bathsheba, realized this. His repentance is found in Psalm 51:4.

Against you, you only, have I sinned and done what is evil in your sight; so you are right in your verdict and justified when you judge.

WE ARE MORE VULNERABLE TO AN ATTACK AFTER WE HAVE SUCCESSFULLY RESISTED THE PREVIOUS ATTACK!

Having sex with anyone who is not your married partner is sin against God. I can't put it any more bluntly. Whether it is premarital sex or an affair, it is sin. It goes against God's perfect design of sex being only between a husband and wife. This is God's order for family life.

To have premarital sex or an affair is to be anti-family and anti-God. It is cheating on the wife you took a sacred vow with on your wedding day. Single guys, sex before marriage is cheating on your future spouse, the same as if you had an affair while married to her. As men, we have a responsibility to stay sexually pure.

There is more to being sexually pure than not actually having sex. Jesus says in Matthew 5:27–28:

*You have heard that it was said, "You shall not commit adultery."
But I tell you that anyone who looks at a woman lustfully has already committed adultery with her in his heart.*

Many men see this as an impossible standard. They feel they have
a right to look at a pretty girl and fantasize about her. However, Jesus
makes it clear. You don't. If we look at a woman lustfully, if we fantasize about a woman, if we masturbate, it is sin against God. There is no
way around it. That is God's rule.

The good news is we have examples in life that show us that sexual
purity can be achieved. Like Joseph, we can refuse to sin against God
by refusing to give in to sexual sin.

The third reason Joseph was able to refuse Mrs. Potiphar's advances
was that he did not want to destroy God's reputation.

It says clearly in the passage that God is responsible for Joseph's
success. He knew it. Potiphar knew it. If he committed this outrageous
sin, he would have taken this praise away from God. Potiphar would
have thought he was just like all other men. He would no longer have
recognized that Joseph's God made people different.

WE MUST RESIST THE OPPORTUNITIES TO SIN

It was not smooth sailing for Joseph after he refused Mrs. Potiphar's
advances. Why? She was a very persistent woman. As we examine the
Scripture we read:

*And though she spoke to Joseph day after day, he refused to go to
bed with her or even be with her.*

This is an important lesson to learn, not only about sexual temptation, but all temptation: **We are more vulnerable to an attack after
we have successfully resisted the previous attack.**

Joseph had just taken a stand for righteousness and integrity. Satan doesn't like that and will come at us harder than before. That is why it is important to always be aware that at any given moment we are vulnerable to temptation. Everything inside of us is programmed to give in to sin. It is what is natural to us. Through the power of God and the willingness on our part to fight, we can be free to be a holy, pure man of integrity.

There is a basic truth we need to understand. As a Christian, there are two forces trying to kill us. They want to destroy everything about us. Satan wants to completely destroy our lives, our relationships, basically everything we have. His goal is to kill us and have us spend eternity in hell with him and his demons.

God is also out to kill us. However, he is doing it for our good. He wants to kill the sinful man inside of us. His purpose is to go after the sinful behavior and tendencies living inside each one of us, whether taught or inherited, so that we become like Jesus. He doesn't want sin ruling us.

He knows we are fallen, sinful men, and wants his very best for us in life just like he wanted for Joseph. This is why God allows temptation to attack us. Satan tempts us to destroy us, but God allows it so we can fight and overcome and become like Jesus.

It is important for us to realize we can fall at any time. We must use this information to prepare ourselves so when the attack comes, we can fight back and overcome.

This principle is in the story of Joseph. Joseph's victory over sexual temptation with Mrs. Potiphar could have made him become proud, but it didn't. He realized his victory was only because of God. He determined in his heart how to withstand her advances toward him.

Can you imagine how hard this was for Joseph as he everyday refused her advances? He was a young man. He was a virgin. He was far away from his family and friends. He was lonely. He felt rejected. His older brothers had just sold him as a slave. He had sexual desires. He could have very easily found comfort in the arms of this more-than-willing woman. Yet he didn't. How did he do it?

He stayed away from her. He didn't let himself get caught in any situation where the temptation could get to him. Let's look at the passage:

And though she spoke to Joseph day after day, he refused to go to bed with her or even be with her.

The NKJV says it this way: *So it was, as she spoke to Joseph day by day, that he did not heed her, to lie with her or to be with her.*

Not only did Joseph refuse to sleep with her, but he refused to even be around her. He knew the limits of his strength and ability to resist her. He knew that he would need a battle plan. This is also true for us. We need to take action and draw up a personal plan before the temptation ever occurs.

The first step in Joseph's plan was to identify his areas of weakness and take steps to overcome them. He refused to be alone in the same room with her. This is key to overcoming sexual temptation. We need to stop and analyze what things are temptations for us. We must study ourselves and identify the areas that are vulnerable to attack.

After we identify our weaknesses, we need to think of ways to overcome them. There is no weakness that can't be conquered. God's strength is made perfect in our weakness.

Find a solution. If watching sensual TV or movies is a problem, take action. One way I have found to do this is through the V-chip. It isn't just for kids. In our home, we block out any TV that is rated higher than PG. Have someone else take charge of the passcode. If you don't know it, you can't use it.

If the Internet is your problem, buy the Covenant Eyes program or similar program that not only blocks porn but also informs your accountability partner of exactly what you are viewing. Every problem has a solution if we will take the time to study ourselves and prepare ahead of time.

For all the single guys reading this book, when dating we must be careful not to put ourselves into situations where our guard may drop. Don't go to secluded places to talk, like a hilltop overlooking a panoramic view. Don't go park somewhere alone to talk. Don't go to each other's residences and be alone in the house.

There are plenty of ways to date and be among people. You can go to a restaurant and have a good conversation. You can go for a walk and talk. The old cliché date of sitting on a front porch talking is safe. You can be alone and still be out among people. Be creative. It will protect you and your date. This keeps away any hint of temptation.

We have learned from Joseph how to refuse to sin sexually. We learned how to create a battle plan ahead of time to resist opportunities to sin. Now we see the third lesson. When we are face to face with sexual temptations, **run like a track star on steroids!**

WE MUST RUN AWAY FROM TEMPTATION

One day he went into the house to attend to his duties, and none of the household servants was inside. She caught him by his cloak and said, "Come to bed with me!" But he left his cloak in her hand and ran out of the house.

Joseph repeatedly refused to sleep with Mrs. Potiphar. However, this day was different. As Joseph arrived at work, he noticed a strange silence in the house. No one was there.

Mrs. Potiphar had set a trap for Joseph. She was determined. She came up behind him and grabbed him. She seductively breathed out, "Lie with me." She wouldn't take no for an answer.

The only thing that was left for Joseph to do was run. Who cared about his success? Who cared about his position? Who cares if he hurt her feelings; he had to get out of there!

This is manliness in its truest form. He knew his limitations. He wasn't proud in thinking he could handle it. He didn't try to consider reasoning with her. Enough was enough. As a living example of the words of the apostle Paul, he "fled from sexual immorality" (I Corinthians 6:18).

Whenever the New Testament discusses the subject of sensual temptation, it gives one command: RUN! The Bible does not tell us to reason with it. It tells us to FLEE!

> **WE CANNOT YIELD TO SENSUALITY IF WE ARE RUNNING AWAY FROM IT!**

We cannot yield to sensuality if we are running away from it.

Run for your life. Get out of there! If we try to reason with lust or entertain sexual thoughts, we will give in to them. We won't be able to fight it. This is why God forcefully orders us to run away from it. This is exactly the way Joseph handled it.

This is the one situation where a godly man should not stand up and fight. With all other temptations we have to bring the boom and conquer it. But not sexual temptation. It is a losing battle. Run with all your might.

It doesn't matter how we look. As Joseph ran away from her, she pulled his cloak off his body. He put the embarrassment of being naked aside and ran. This is what we need to do. After we refuse to sin, and resist opportunities to sin, we must run.

A FINAL WARNING

The above lesson is vital for all men to learn and master. We need to stop falling for Satan's traps. However, as Joseph's life shows us, it may cost us.

> *When she saw that he had left his cloak in her hand and had run out of the house, she called her household servants. "Look," she said to them, "this Hebrew has been brought to us to make sport of us! He came in here to sleep with me, but I screamed. When he heard me scream for help, he left his cloak beside me and ran out of the house."*

> *She kept his cloak beside her until his master came home. Then she told him this story: "That Hebrew slave you brought us came to me to make sport of me. But as soon as I screamed for help, he left his cloak beside me and ran out of the house."*

> *When his master heard the story his wife told him, saying, "This is how your slave treated me," he burned with anger. Joseph's master took him and put him in prison, the place where the king's prisoners were confined.*

Outraged at Joseph's denial, she sought revenge. She created a lie that made it appear that she was a victim of Joseph. As a result, Joseph lost everything: his job, his success, and his freedom. He was put in jail and left to rot.

You are probably thinking, "That's not fair. He did the right thing. Why did God allow this to happen? Why should I fight like Joseph if this is the outcome?"

These are good questions.

Doing the right thing could cost us. It could cost clients, our jobs, or our friends. However, if we do what is right, God *will* vindicate us. Suffering for doing right is a much better option than what could happen if we don't resist the temptation. Let me tell you a story to illustrate this point.

Once there was a young man who was walking home late at night. He gave no thought to his ways. He never took the time to examine himself and see what areas opened him up to sexual sin. He wasn't careful to avoid situations that allowed him to be tempted. He was naive.

As he was walking home, he was met by a beautiful woman. She was dressed seductively. She knew exactly what to say to the man to get him to come home with her.

She walks up to him, grabs him, and kisses him. She looks at him seductively and says, "Come home with me. We can make love. I am a good, religious woman. It's okay. I came looking just for you. I have had my eye on you. Now I found you. Come back to my place. I have the mood set with scented candles and soft music. No one will know. My husband is away on business and won't be back for a few days. Come on! Let's go!"

> **WHEN FACE TO FACE WITH SEXUAL TEMPTATION, RUN LIKE A TRACK STAR ON STEROIDS!**

She talked him into it. He had no prearranged plan, no means to resist. He didn't run. He was trapped. He didn't escape.

You may recognize this story as being from Proverbs 7. This man didn't take the necessary steps that Joseph took in the same situation. Joseph suffered some jail time before being vindicated and honored by God. What happened to the other young man?

All at once he followed her like an ox going to the slaughter, like a deer stepping into a noose till an arrow pierces his liver, like a bird darting into a snare, little knowing it will cost him his life.

Now then, my sons, listen to me; pay attention to what I say. Do not let your heart turn to her ways or stray into her paths. Many are the victims she has brought down; her slain are a mighty throng. Her house is a highway to the grave, leading down to the chambers of death.

He went to hell. Satan managed to trap him and kill him. When Satan kills you, he doesn't resurrect you. He keeps you dead in hell for all of eternity.

These are important stakes. We have two choices. The first choice is to refuse to change and give in to sexual sin. If we make this choice, we will open ourselves up to be destroyed by Satan.

Our other choice is to refuse to sin. We must make a conscious effort to examine ourselves. We must make a victory plan. We have to run away from temptation. These choices will be blessed by God. The choice is clear and the choice is ours. In my opinion, the latter is the only choice for a godly man. So choose today to develop a legacy of sexual purity.

Dear heavenly Father, please forgive me for any time I have committed any form of sexual sin against you, whether it be masturbation, pornography, sex outside of marriage, or even looking at a girl lustfully. Cleanse my mind from the damage I have done to it through these sexual sins. Help me to change my behavior in these areas. Help me to develop a battle plan to overcome these temptations, and help me to be man enough to run when any sexual temptation may come. I want to be a man committed to sexual purity. In Jesus' name, amen.

LEGACY CHALLENGES

1. Identify the areas of your life that cause you to be tempted to sin sexually. Write down a clear battleplan to overcome.

2. Take a sheet of paper and, through the power of the Holy Spirit, identify times you have sinned sexually. Include any TV shows, movies, magazines, thoughts, and actions. Then spend time in prayer confessing these sins to God. Ask him to forgive you. Ask God to restore your mind to purity and holiness like his. Begin to live a pure and holy life before God.

3. In the future, keep a short account with God. Anytime a thought to sin sexually enters your mind, cast it down in Jesus' name. Confess it and move on, continuing the pursuit of sexual purity.

EXTREME LEGACY CHALLENGES

1. For one month do not watch any TV or any movies. Instead take that time and spend it reading the Bible. You will be surprised at the end of the month how little your conscience will allow you to watch after renewing your mind.

2. Begin using the V-chip on your TV and install a Internet filtering program on your computer. Have someone else set the override passwords.

3. Read *Every Man's Battle* and *Tactics* By Fred Stoeker.

GROUP STUDY QUESTIONS

1. When was the first time you were exposed to pornography or sexual temptation? What do you remember thinking or feeling in that moment?

2. How is society's view of a real man and God's view of sexual purity different?

3. What part of this chapter stood out to you the most? What area needs the most work?

4. What are your thoughts on the idea that both Satan and God are trying to kill you?

5. How do you feel about Jesus' statement that looking at a woman lustfully is the same as having sex with her?

6. How does the idea that a real man runs away from spiritual temptation instead of staying and reasoning sound to you?

7. How can a V-chip for your TV help you?

8. Do you think the idea of not being alone with a woman is a good idea or not? Why?

9. What may taking a stand cost you? What will not taking a stand cost you?

10. What is your final decision, to be like Joseph or like the man in Proverbs 7?

9

THE BOAZ LEGACY

BECOMING A LADIES' MAN

Ladies' man—this is a phrase that I have come to hate!

In fact, it infuriates me!

Our society's view of a ladies' man is warped and twisted, and too many of God's men have bought into the lie. But instead of ranting about it, I decided to add a chapter to this book and discuss what it means for a man of God to be a ladies' man—a.k.a., how a man of God should treat God's precious daughters.

Single guys, listen up; this chapter is dedicated to you as we look at a single man in the Bible and the tremendous legacy he has left for us all to follow. Married guys, don't skip over this chapter—there is something for all of us to learn from Boaz's legacy as we daily interact with the other half of the population, God's precious daughters.

Boaz is an incredible example for us all to study. He is an extraordinary model to us all. Other than Jesus, I can't think of a better man than Boaz to show us how to be a godly man that all women can love and respect.

Boaz lived in the period of Israel's history known as "The Judges." This was the time just after Israel had taken possession of their Promised Land. Joshua, their righteous leader, had just died. This was not Israel's greatest moment in history. It is summarized by the phrase repeated throughout the book of Judges, *"The people did what was right in their own eyes."*

Over and over, the book of Judges shows a downward spiral among God's people. The people would abandon God and his ways, God would send an enemy to attack and oppress them, and they would cry out to God for deliverance. Each time God would have mercy on them and send them a judge to deliver them, men like Ehud, Samson, Othniel and a woman, Deborah. However, once set free, the people would return to their old way of life and abandon the ways of God, starting the pattern over and over.

It was in these circumstances that Boaz lived and worked. However, he wasn't like the rest of the people. He was a rare man in his day. He was different. He lived a righteous life before God. He loved God and lived to please him. He followed God's commandments.

We see this in the way he treated Ruth, a poor widow Moabite woman who had left her nation and people and had moved to the nation of Israel with her mother-in-law. As we examine the story of Boaz and Ruth, we will learn how a godly man should treat the women around him. We will learn some key ways to treat women, ensuring we will have stronger, more meaningful relationships as we become the godly men the women around us want and deserve. We will see that Boaz protected Ruth, he respected her character, he was honest with her, and he understood her needs and helped her.

BOAZ PROTECTED RUTH

Boaz understood a fact that many men today don't understand. It is our job to protect the women God has place in our lives. That's the very first lesson we learn from Boaz: He was a man that woman could count on to protect them. Let me explain.

In the Old Testament, God gave a command for his people to help supply the needs of widows. One way of doing this was to supply food for them. When a farmer harvested his crops, he was forbidden from completely scraping the field clean. Instead, he was supposed to leave remnants of the food for the poor and widows.

In Boaz's day, few farmers obeyed this command. Not only that, but quite often the men would harass and assault widows if they found them gleaning in their field. However, Boaz was different. He did it God's way.

For example, one day, Boaz observed a woman, Ruth, gleaning in his field. Instead of harassing her or abusing her, he made sure she was safe and protected.

So Boaz said to Ruth, "My daughter, listen to me. Don't go and glean in another field and don't go away from here. Stay here with my servant girls. Watch the field where the men are harvesting, and follow along after the girls. I have told the men not to touch you. And whenever you are thirsty, go and get a drink from the water jars the men have filled" (Ruth 2:8).

Boaz made sure that no harm came to Ruth. He provided her with other people to protect her, he made sure no one could attack her or take advantage of her in the fields. He even made sure she didn't become dehydrated by making sure she got plenty of water to drink while working in the hot Israeli sun. We need to learn from Boaz's example and make sure we do all we can to protect the women God has blessed us with.

I know I personally had to learn this lesson. I grew up with a dad who never protected my mom or sister. He allowed anyone to come against them and never took their side. I saw this and learned his sinful behavior. However, God taught me how to be more protective of them and how to make them feel safer.

People can attack me or say what they want about me, but look out if they do it to my sister! This is the responsibility of all godly men. We must allow the women in our lives to have the privilege of protection, safety, and security.

This applies not only to our fellow sisters in Christ. Ruth was not an Israelite. She was not one of God's people. But Boaz treated her just like he did his fellow Israelites. What an awesome testimony for a man of God!

BOAZ APPRECIATED RUTH FOR HER CHARACTER, NOT HER APPEARANCE

Many men today are guilty of placing our attention on the physical appearance of the women around us. We judge them based on their beauty and sexual appeal. This is wrong. Boaz demonstrates to us what we should learn to appreciate about women.

> *At this, she bowed down with her face to the ground. She exclaimed, "Why have I found such favor in your eyes that you notice me—a foreigner?"*
>
> *Boaz replied, "I've been told all about what you have done for your mother-in-law since the death of your husband—how you left your father and mother and your homeland and came to live with a people you did not know before. May the LORD repay you for what you have done. May you be richly rewarded by the LORD, the God of Israel, under whose wings you have come to take refuge."*

Notice Boaz doesn't equate Ruth's value in terms of her physical appearance. The first time he met her she was dirty and sweaty from picking grain all day. Her hair and clothes were most likely a mess and she more than likely smelled horrible.

However, Boaz appreciated Ruth's character and integrity. Later in the book he tells her she is a woman of noble character. Boaz understood that beauty is fleeting, but a woman who fears God should be valued. He appreciated Ruth for who she was, not how she looked. We need to do the same.

God does not want us to choose a wife based on her appearance. The world directs us to see women this way. Is she pretty? Is she sexy? Would she win me the approval of my friends?

> **GOD WANTS HIS MEN TO UNDERSTAND THAT CHARACTER AND INNER BEAUTY ARE THE BASIS OF RELATIONSHIPS, NOT APPEARANCE.**

The world looks at girls as trophies, not human beings. They place value on their physical appearance, not their character. This is sin. God wants his men to understand that character and inner beauty are the basis of relationships, not appearance.

We need to look at women through God's eyes. Physical appearance should not be the determining factor of who we will and will not date. God wants us looking at a woman's heart to see her character and integrity. These need to be the things that attract us to women. If this is not our basis, then we have some changes to make.

Again, this was an area I had to examine in myself and make changes. Because of my disability and because of the abuse I suffered in life, I struggled tremendously with insecurity and never feeling like a real man.

One way I looked to deal with this was to prove I was a real man by having a stunningly beautiful girlfriend. I was a complete jerk who only looked at a woman's outward appearance until God showed me how this was sinful, and I had to repent. I can honestly say to you today God has transformed me so that what attracts me to a woman now is her heart for God and her desire to serve him, not her physical appearance. How did I get to this place? How do you make these changes?

The first thing we need to do is to repent. Ask God to forgive you for viewing women through the world's eyes instead of through his.

Then make a list of every time you have done this in your life. Examine why you did it. Face your insecurities and your desire to have a beautiful girl on your arm to make yourself feel good about yourself.

Then ask God to change you and help you no longer commit this sin.

Ask God to change your heart so you are attracted to a woman's walk with God and her inner spirit. Ask him to heal your inner soul from the sickness of valuing women based on their appearance. Beg him to help you view women through his eyes. Follow Boaz's example and begin viewing women through God's eyes, seeing their beauty in their character and relationship with God.

BOAZ WAS OPEN AND HONEST WITH RUTH

So far we have read how Boaz obeyed God's laws by supplying for Ruth and any other widow's needs. Ruth continued returning day after day to Boaz's field. Every night, she took back what she picked to supply her mother-in-law, Naomi. Naomi loved Ruth and wanted her to be happy, so she told Ruth about the Israelite law of kinsman redeemers.

According to this law, when an Israelite man died, his closest kin was responsible to marry and provide for the dead man's widow. As an Israelite convert, Ruth had a kinsmen redeemer. It was Boaz. Naomi told Ruth to go to Boaz and ask him to fulfill his duty and marry her. Ruth did just that.

She obeyed Naomi's instructions and told Boaz that he was her kinsmen redeemer. As we read Boaz's response we see a man of honor and integrity.

All the people of my town know that you are a woman of noble character. Although it is true that I am a guardian-redeemer of our family, there is another who is more closely related than I. Stay here for the night, and in the morning if he wants to do his duty as your guardian-redeemer, good; let him redeem. But if he is not willing, as surely as the LORD lives I will do it.

I believe Boaz had fallen in love with Ruth and her incredible character. He wanted to be her kinsmen redeemer, but he didn't know if he could.

Notice he was open and honest with her. He didn't lead her on or give her false hope. He was completely upfront by explaining the circumstances. He didn't lie or deceive her. This is key for all men to learn.

Nothing kills a relationship faster than deceit. No relationship can withstand lies. They destroy trust. Deceit gives ground to suspicion.

As godly men, we must be completely honest with women and let them know exactly what is going on. We cannot lie or hide things, even if we think it is for their own good. We must trust them enough to be open and transparent about everything, and we need to answer any questions they may have. Whether it relate to finances, work, or our relationship, we must always be open and honest with women.

> **AS GODLY MEN, WE MUST BE COMPLETELY HONEST WITH WOMEN. WE MUST TRUST THEM AND BE OPEN, HONEST, AND TRANSPARENT WITH THEM.**

Boaz immediately went to the other guy and took care of things. He told the other kinsmen redeemer about Ruth, and when the other man refused to marry Ruth, Boaz kept his word. He married Ruth. However, we can't skip through the conclusion of this story too fast. We must notice one more thing.

BOAZ REALIZED THAT RUTH'S NEEDS AND DESIRES WERE IMPORTANT AND DESERVED HIS IMMEDIATE ATTENTION

I recently saw a post on Facebook that said, "Ladies, if a man said he will fix it, he will. There is no need to remind him every six months about it!"

While a funny post, it is also a grim reminder of how often we as men don't take the concerns and desires of the women in our lives very seriously. Boaz sets an awesome example of how we should react when women present something to us that is important to them. Boaz took Ruth's request for him to be her kinsmen redeemer seriously.

Then Naomi said, "Wait, my daughter, until you find out what happens. For the man will not rest until the matter is settled today. …Meanwhile Boaz went up to the town gate and sat there just as the guardian-redeemer he had mentioned came along, Boaz said, "Come over here, my friend, and sit down."

He knew this was important to Ruth, so he dealt with it immediately. I am sure he had things to do and business to take care of, but he put her issues ahead of his. He didn't want her to have to stress and worry about it any longer than was necessary, so he dropped everything to do what Ruth wanted done.

I don't know about you, but this is tremendously convicting to me. God has been showing me that far too often I put off the concerns and worries of women. I put my own responsibilities ahead of theirs. I hate being interrupted when I am in the middle of something, and far too often I blow off others and what they need.

I can no longer do this. I need to follow Boaz's example and become a servant to women, no matter what they want and when they want it. I must stop what I am doing and give them my attention and help. Women deserve our time and attention and we need to give it to them.

Boaz was an extraordinary man and an excellent example for us all. He shows us some great areas to work on and improve ourselves so we can have good, healthy, and godly relationships in our lives. Boaz was a *real* ladies' man because he treated women with dignity and respect. He treated them as what they really are, daughters of the Almighty God. He left behind an amazing legacy for us all to strive for in our lives.

Dear heavenly Father, thank you for including Boaz's legacy in the Bible. I too want to become a man who treats your daughters the way they deserve to be treated, with dignity and respect.

Please forgive me for every time I treated your daughters in an ungodly way, following the model of the world. Help me from this day forward to start a new legacy that treats women with respect, that sees the true beauty of a woman, that is open and honest with women, and that puts her concerns and desires ahead of my own. In Jesus' name, amen.

LEGACY CHALLENGES

Sit down with a piece of paper and write down all the ways you can think of that society defines a ladies' man.

Then make another list of what the Bible says about the first list you made. Then repent of times you followed society's view.

EXTREME LEGACY CHALLENGES

Take the second list you just made of how the Bible contradicts the world's view of a ladies' man. Then use a concordance or an online search to find a verse in the Bible that directly contradicts the world's lies of how to view women. Memorize the verse.

GROUP STUDY QUESTIONS

1. This chapter discussed how Boaz interacted with and treated Ruth. What does the fact that Ruth was not an Israelite tell us about how God's men should treat unsaved women?

2. Of the four points discussed in this chapter, which are you strongest in doing?

3. Of the four points discussed in this chapter, in which area do you struggle the most?

4. How can deceit affect relationships?

5. We mentioned that men need to put the desires of women ahead of our own. Why is this so hard for men to do?

6. How do we overcome and do it?

7. How can we as a group help each other apply the lesson from Boaz's legacy to our lives?

10

THE MORDECAI LEGACY

BECOMING A
RESPONSIBLE MAN

In this chapter, we are going to discuss a legacy which scares many men. It is something many men avoid, few embrace, but all should develop. It's one of the true signs of a growing, godly man. Any man who wants to reach his full potential must develop it. If you want a happy marriage (whether now, if you're married, or in the future, if you're single), you must accept it. If you want your children to become mature adults, you must teach it. If your heart's desire is to be a godly man, you must embrace it. What is this quality? It is *responsibility*.

RESPONSI-WHAT?

Too often men struggle to say the word *responsibility*, similar to how Fonzie struggled to say he was wrong. (Yes, this reference shows my age. If you're too young to get it, look it up on YouTube.)

Responsibility is defined as a thing which one is required to do as part of a job, role, or legal obligation. A responsible person is accountable for his behavior. He is capable of being trusted. He is reliable and dependable. He exhibits good judgment and sound thinking. He is involved in important duties and decisions. He willingly accepts these things and pursues them on his own. We must become mature men who can take care of things and be responsible.

There seems to be a growing trend in our society for men to let women handle everything for them. Men are becoming more involved in playing and activities, leaving the bulk of responsibilities to women. Churches, businesses, and political positions are being filled by women because men are shirking their responsibilities.

I want to make one thing clear. I am not a chauvinist pig. I have no problem with women ministering or being involved with politics. I believe women should be able to do whatever they want to do. However, *want* is the key word. They should *desire* to do it. They shouldn't be forced to do it because men aren't willing to be steady, dependable men who take care of their own responsibilities. We need to address this area.

As men, we need to accept responsibility in all areas of life. Some men may be financially responsible, but at the same time, be completely emotionally irresponsible. Other men may be able to give emotional support, yet they fail to handle their day-to-day household responsibilities. Being a responsible, dependable man is a goal we should strive to achieve in every area of our lives.

Growing up and in my early days of manhood, I never volunteered to take on responsibility. If someone needed a man to hang out with, I was there. If they needed a golfing partner, I was all up for that. If they wanted to play the latest video game, I was stoked. However, if they needed someone to help them take care of their yard or paint a room, I usually made myself scarce.

I was irresponsible financially. I used my money for my entertainment needs. I didn't budget or save. If I had money, I spent it.

Emotionally, I was totally irresponsible. I never reached out and helped people when they were hurting and needed help. I was all up for fun and good times, but was not dependable during the hard, painful times. Usually, I handled these times by telling a joke or changing the subject. However, God began to show me my weakness in these areas in an effort to develop responsibility within me.

God taught me that a godly man willingly accepts responsibility. As a matter of fact, he will take the initiative and seek out opportunities to be responsible. He is mature and responsible in all facets of life. He is a man you can depend on in time of need.

The next man we are going to study has a stellar legacy of being a responsible man. His name is Mordecai, and he demonstrates for us the need to become men who are willing to accept responsibility.

A MODEL OF RESPONSIBILITY

Mordecai lived during the period of time when the nation of Israel was exiled in Babylon. After the seventy years had passed, some of the Jews were allowed to return to Jerusalem. However, Mordecai was not one of them. He lived in Shushan, the fortress of King Ahasuerus, and worked as a gatekeeper, or a doorman, at the king's palace.

Mordecai was no stranger to responsibility. He didn't run from it. Instead, he embraced it. When he was around twenty years old, his family experienced a horrible tragedy. His uncle and aunt died, leaving a small daughter behind. At this point, we see the first time Mordecai stepped up and accepted responsibility.

Mordecai had a cousin named Hadassah, whom he had brought up because she had neither father nor mother. This young woman, who was also known as Esther, had a lovely figure and was beauti-

ful. Mordecai had taken her as his own daughter when her father and mother died (Esther 2:7).

Mordecai saw the helpless little girl who was all alone in the world and did what any godly man should do. He took her into his home and raised her. He took responsibility for her. He clothed her, protected her, and took care of all of her needs. She became his daughter.

Notice that nowhere does the passage say Mordecai was married. There was no wife to pass the responsibilities of childcare to. He did it himself. All Mordecai knew was the little girl needed a father and he was the next of kin. He manned up and took responsibility for young Hadassah.

As we continue through the book of Esther, we find Mordecai never stopped caring for Hadassah, even when she is fully grown. This was no easy task when Hadassah found herself in a horrible position.

The king was in search of a new queen. In a drunken stupor, the king decided to banish his queen, and now he found himself alone.

Trying to find a solution to the problem he created, the king made a decree which made every beautiful girl in his nation part of his harem. Each girl was presented to the king until he found one that pleased him.

> **A GODLY MAN DOESN'T LEAVE OR ABANDON— HE STAYS!**

Unfortunately for Hadassah, she was a very beautiful girl. She was chosen to become a part of the king's harem.

This must have broken Mordecai's heart. As the king's gatekeeper, he knew the horrors these girls experienced. Now his little girl, his adopted daughter, was to become one of them. Again, we see Mordecai's fatherly sense of responsibility kick in.

Every day he walked back and forth near the courtyard of the harem to find out how Esther was and what was happening to her.

Daily, Mordecai went and checked on Hadassah, whose name was now changed to Esther. He made sure she was okay. He gave her council and instruction on how to handle her new life. He never stopped taking care of her and being concerned for her.

Eventually, her night with the king came, and afterward the king chose her to be his queen. Even after this new development, Mordecai kept in constant contact with Esther. He never stopped taking responsibility for her.

We need to follow Mordecai's example. We need to take responsibility for the family God has given to us. A godly man doesn't leave or abandon—he stays! We need to be men who are always putting the safety and welfare of our family first. We must always be aware of their needs and do all we can to take care of them, whether the needs be physical, spiritual, material, or emotional. A godly man will want to take this responsibility for his family.

As we continue, we see that Mordecai not only took responsibility for his family, Esther, but he also takes care of his employer, the king.

During the time Mordecai was sitting at the king's gate, Bigthana and Teresh, two of the king's officers who guarded the doorway, became angry and conspired to assassinate King Xerxes. But Mordecai found out about the plot and told Queen Esther, who in turn reported it to the king, giving credit to Mordecai. And when the report was investigated and found to be true, the two officials were impaled on poles. All this was recorded in the book of the annals in the presence of the king.

Mordecai was a faithful employee. He didn't just do what was necessary to get by, but he went the extra mile. He gave his boss all he had to give. When Mordecai learned of the plot to murder the king, he immediately stepped up and stopped it. As a result, the king's life was spared.

God wants us to be responsible with the jobs he gives us to do. Unfortunately, we live in a society where many people don't care about their work. They are content to just pick up a paycheck as they work for the weekend. Quality of merchandise has dropped. Customer service has decreased. Many have abandoned the idea of being a responsible employee. This attitude is not pleasing to God.

In my past, I've had a bad behavioral pattern in which I do my work as fast as I can so I can get back to what I want to do. God showed me this is sin. He taught me that I need to do a job well. I had to learn to take pride in my work and make sure that any job I am given is done properly.

I couldn't continue to do things part-way or have poor workmanship. I needed to take my time and do a good job. Now I drive people crazy as I strive to make everything just right, no matter how long it takes!

GOD NEVER GETS TIRED OF STRETCHING US. HE WANTS US TO BE DEPENDABLE MEN WHO CAN BE TRUSTED WITH MORE AND MORE.

God wants all of us to be responsible workers. He wants us to do all we can to help our employers and companies. When we are responsible with our jobs, we are good examples for God. We will stand out among the crowd. People will see that we are different, and God will receive praise because of our actions.

As we grow into men who can be depended upon to take care of those God has given to us, we will find that God starts to stretch us and give us more responsibilities.

God never gets tired of stretching us. He wants us to be dependable men who can be trusted with more and more. God did this with Mordecai. First, Mordecai accepted responsibility for Esther. Then God put him in a situation where he took responsibility for the king. As we continue on through Mordecai's life, we see God continues to stretch him.

The king had a man working for him named Haman. Haman was a proud, arrogant, self-seeking man who was searching for power and authority. As he ascended through the ranks of the royal court, he became even more power-hungry. We read in the book of Esther that Haman eventually reached a position where he expected all the people to bow down to him. It is at this point that we see Mordecai's responsibilities increase.

> *But Mordecai would not kneel down or pay him honor. Then the royal officials at the king's gate asked Mordecai, "Why do you disobey the king's command?" Day after day they spoke to him but he refused to comply. Therefore they told Haman about it to see whether Mordecai's behavior would be tolerated, for he had told them he was a Jew.*
>
> *When Haman saw that Mordecai would not kneel down or pay him honor, he was enraged.*

Mordecai refused to bow down to Haman because Mordecai was a devoted Jew. He bowed to no one but God. He took responsibility for his walk with God. He made sure that he had no sin in his life and stayed loyal to God. He didn't make anyone else be his moral compass. He knew what he believed and refused to bend.

Haman became outraged and sought revenge.

> *Yet having learned who Mordecai's people were, he scorned the idea of killing only Mordecai. Instead Haman looked for a way to destroy all Mordecai's people, the Jews, throughout the whole kingdom of Xerxes.*

Satan hates to see us become strong, dependable, responsible men. The minute he sees us begin to move in this direction, he will attack us. He wants to stop us. He wants to kill us. He definitely doesn't want us to become like Jesus.

In this passage we see that Mordecai faced an attack designed to stop his maturing. As you seek to become a responsible man, trust me, the attack will come. You need to be prepared for the attack and fight through it. As a result, character will be developed and more responsibility will be earned. This is exactly what happened to Mordecai.

Haman devised a plan to destroy all the Jews. He tricked the king into making a decree that permitted a total annihilation of all Israel. Unknown to the king, the decree included his own queen, Esther.

When Mordecai heard of this horrible decree, he was heartbroken. Immediately, he went into mourning, covering himself in ashes.

Esther soon learned of Mordecai's actions. However, she didn't know the reason. Here we see Mordecai's responsibilities stretched even further as he takes responsibility for the entire nation of Israel.

Mordecai devised a plan to save all the Jews. He asked Esther to approach the king and tell him of Haman's evil plan.

Mordecai's bold plan put Esther's life in danger. No one approached the king without the king sending for them. If you did, you could be killed. However, Mordecai knew he had to help his nation, so he asked Esther to take the risk.

Much to her credit, she did. As a result, she convinced the king to not allow the Jews to be killed. Instead, the king ordered Haman to die and then the king took measures to save the Jews.

You would think at this point that the aging Mordecai would sit back and let other people handle things for awhile. However, the exact opposite happens.

And all his acts of power and might, together with a full account of the greatness of Mordecai, whom the king had promoted, are they not written in the book of the annals of the kings of Media and Persia? Mordecai the Jew was second in rank to King Xerxes, preeminent among the Jews, and held in high esteem by his many fellow Jews, because he worked for the good of his people and spoke up for the welfare of all the Jews (Esther 10:1–3).

We read that Mordecai is stretched once again. He is now put in a position where he is responsible for the entire Persian Empire, second only to the king. It is important to remember that this was the dominant world empire during this time. Mordecai's position was equal to our vice president. He had come a long way from the first step of raising his orphaned cousin.

That's what God loves to do: take a man who is willing to grow and stretch him into a strong, responsible, dependable person.

LEARNING RESPONSIBILITY

As we wrap up this chapter, I want to take a moment and be open about this area of becoming a responsible man. I mentioned in the beginning of this chapter that I was a man who avoided responsibilities. I always enjoyed having fun instead of working around the house. A few years ago, God began showing me how sinful this was.

When I didn't pick up my responsibilities, they were passed on to other people. They were overloaded with things to handle. They were forced to be responsible for all the financial decisions. A majority of the work and planning of projects was dumped on them. They had to make decisions. They did many things they never should have had to do. I was sinning against them by causing them so much stress and anxiety. I had to repent to them and God and make changes in my life. I had to begin pursuing responsibility.

God started me off slowly and consistently gave me more and more responsibility. He helped me to grow as I learned to do new things. He gave me the wisdom and strength to learn new ways and develop new patterns.

God faithfully helped me grow into a responsible, godly man.

I remember back about ten years ago when God taught me to be responsible financially. I learned the benefits of a budget. He taught me to work with the family and responsibly use money for family needs. He showed me how to be responsible by keeping accurate financial records. I learned to be financially accountable to those around me.

I have been stretched emotionally. God required me to be more open and honest with my emotions. He taught me how to have relationships with people and to handle their emotions. I learned to be more supportive. I have learned to be vulnerable and share parts of myself with people that I would normally keep to myself for fear of rejection.

I try to no longer make jokes or change the subject on emotionally painful topics. I am trying to be more sensitive and compassionate. Most important, I learned how to choose my feelings and not allow my emotions to control me. I have not arrived, but I am working toward godliness in these areas. As a result, God is growing me into a mature, capable, responsible man.

Each day it seems he presents me with a new, exciting opportunity to develop even more. Just in the past year, we brought out a book, formed a 501c3, and started a new branch of ministry, causing me to be stretched in how to run these things, how to handle the finances, how to prepare and plan, and how to make sure the others involved are taken care of and provided for. These are just some of many areas where I've been stretched. I sometimes joke that God's nickname for me must be Taffy because he is always stretching me!

I fully believe that if I hadn't allowed God to stretch me and grow me and increase my levels of responsibilities years ago, he never would have trusted me with the responsibility of running Mantour Ministries. We all have to prove ourselves faithful with the little things in life before God will trust us with the big things. Accepting responsibility is a must for any man who wants to become like Jesus. Allow me to explain.

THE ULTIMATE MODEL OF RESPONSIBILITY

Jesus was the ultimate example of how to be responsible. As a young man, Jesus' stepfather Joseph died. Jesus took over the family business and supported his mother and his siblings. He always took care of them and made sure all their needs were met. Even as he hung on the cross, he made sure that his mother would be provided for and taken care of.

The whole time Jesus was on earth taking care of all these responsibilities, he maintained all of his relationships, especially the one with his heavenly Father. He never forfeited his prayer life. He never stopped seeking God and consulting with him. He totally allowed the Holy Spirit to lead and guide him in every area of his life on earth.

> **JESUS' ENTIRE MISSION ON EARTH WAS GEARED TO TAKING RESPONSIBILITY.**

Jesus' entire mission on earth was geared to taking responsibility. We are all separated from God because of sin. Jesus came to earth with the single purpose of taking responsibility for all the sins of man. He died on the cross in our place. He literally laid down his life for us. We would have no hope of being reconciled with God if Jesus hadn't done this for us. Because of him, we can now experience forgiveness of sin and reconciliation with God.

Jesus' responsibility didn't end there. He faithfully did his saving work on Calvary. Now, he is taking responsibility for us again. Daily, he prays for us and oversees our lives. He is our advocate before God as

Satan daily throws attacks at us. He is always concerned for our well-being.

His responsibility will increase as he later judges the entire world. Everyone will answer to him for the lives they lived. He will then take responsibility for running the new millennium kingdom. Jesus is our model of responsibility. If we want to be like him, we must do the same.

What about you? In what areas are you lacking when it comes to being a responsible, dependable man?

How can you work on taking on more responsibilities?

Maybe you need to be more emotionally supportive to those around you. It could be that you are lacking in the area of financial responsibility. Maybe you haven't been as dependable or reliable a spouse as possible.

What is it causing the irresponsibility?

Is it a pattern you developed as a kid?

Is having fun and relaxing too important in your life? Whatever the reason, you must face it. You must repent of any sins involved. Then you must change.

There are no easy 1-2-3 steps to becoming a responsible man. It is only developed one way: through lots of hard work. You must face the truth about yourself and then begin to do the things you have previously shied away from doing. It can only be done through hard work, perseverance, a desire to change, and most importantly, the power of God.

Ask God to show you the reason for your failure to be a responsible man. Ask him to present you with opportunities to increase your responsibilities. Tell him you want to be a mature, dependable, and responsible man. Then allow him to stretch you and make you into a man who can be given more and more responsibilities. This is the legacy of a responsible, godly man. The question is, are you willing to do it?

Dear heavenly Father, thank you for giving us Jesus as a model of how to handle responsibility. Please forgive me for not being a mature, dependable man. Show me areas in my life that are wrong or sinful in your eyes, the areas that are not your will or your way. I want you to grow and stretch me. Please make me into a man who can be depended upon by those around me no matter what they face in life. Help me as I begin pursuing responsibility. Give me strength to overcome attacks designed to keep me from growing. I choose today to become a responsible, godly man. In Jesus' name, amen.

LEGACY CHALLENGES

1. Make a list of all the areas in your life that you have failed at being responsible. Then repent to God and the people your actions affected. Make a plan on how you can grow in this area.

2. Look for ways to lighten the load on those around you. Step up and help them with their responsibilities.

3. Learn to be financially responsible. If you don't have a budget, make one! Work as a family and develop a budget that everyone can participate in. If you are single, make a budget for yourself and stick to it.

EXTREME LEGACY CHALLENGES

I have found that the people around me can see areas where I am lacking responsibility more clearly than I can. While it is hard to hear, I have found their assessment of me to be very beneficial in areas where I need to grow. Ask the people in your life if they see any areas in which you are irresponsible. Be open to their feedback and make changes.

GROUP STUDY QUESTIONS

1. What is responsibility?

2. Are there areas in your life that need to be stretched so you can be more responsible?

3. How does responsibility relate to your job?

4. How does responsibility relate to your emotions?

5. How does responsibility relate to your finances?

6. How does responsibility relate to your relationships with God and others?

11

THE ELIJAH LEGACY

MENTORING THE
NEXT GENERATION

A few months ago, I saw a commercial that I absolutely loved. It was for the NFL initiative "PLAY 60," and it featured Cam Newton, the quarterback for the Carolina Panthers, and a little boy. Cam was encouraging the little guy to spend time everyday playing outside to get exercise and have fun. Full of enthusiasm, the little boy asks Cam, "I'll grow up to be big and strong like you?"

Cam replied, "Absolutely."

The boy says, "And play in the NFL?"

Cam answered, "Yes, sir!"

"And be drafted number one?"

"Maybe?"

"And become the starting quarterback of the Panthers?"

Cam hesitates and says "Okay." The kid pipes up again, "You can be my back up."

A stunned Cam says, "Excuse me?"

Unfazed, the boy says "And make the Panthers fans forget all about you."

Annoyed, Cam exclaims, "What!"

Undaunted, the boy goes on, "And become your mom's favorite player?"

Cam is flustered and says, "Whoa!" but, still unfazed, the young guy starts rotating his arm around in a throwing motion and says, "I'm just loosening my arm!"

I absolutely love this commercial and this little boy's passion! I laugh every time I see it. This little kid has a number-one-draft-pick-starting-quarterback-superstar worried and intimidated that he will be outdone and replaced! Cam obviously hasn't been taught what we are going to learn today, a lesson all God's men need to hear if we are going to be effective mentors to God's younger men. What is that lesson?

MY GENERATION'S CEILING IS THE NEXT GENERATION'S FLOOR

I love this quote. In my opinion this should be the definition of mentorship. This is the attitude all men of God should adapt in their lives. We should encourage the next generation to surpass us spiritually! We should never discourage them in order to promote ourselves and our interests. A real man of God hopes the next generation goes above and beyond what he is doing and then does all he can to help them do it!

The best men I can think of in the Bible to demonstrate this point are found in 1 Kings. These two men's lives will serve as examples to men of all ages. Basically, they exemplify men in two stages of life. Each of us belongs to one of these groups and some of us may be lucky enough to be in both.

One of the men is a young man starting out his life and his walk with God. The other man is an older man who has been serving God for many years. So as you see, this chapter is relevant to all men, no matter their age.

I want us to look at the lives of Elijah the prophet and his apprentice, Elisha. Talk about confusing! These are two very similar names. (Kind of makes you wonder why God couldn't have Elijah's assistant be named Bob!) We'll just try and keep them straight together.

In the interest of full disclosure and honesty, this chapter was inspired by a sermon I heard at a men's convention. The speaker's message resonated with me, and it has been stirring in my spirit ever since.

Elijah lived during the time of the kings. He was constantly used by God to stand up to the evil King Ahab and to try to get him to stop sinning and become a godly king. Elijah served God faithfully for years, enduring heartache and persecution because of his walk with God. He spent years running for his life as he faithfully served God. We are going to pick up Elijah's story toward the end of his life.

Elijah had just had another run-in with Ahab and his wife, Jezebel. He was feeling discouraged and alone. He questioned God as to why God allowed him to be so persecuted. He felt like he was the only man that was serving God. God spoke to Elijah and told him that he was not alone, that God still had other men serving him. Then God led Elijah past a farm and introduced him to a young man named Elisha who loved God. Let's look at 1 Kings 19:19–21.

So Elijah went from there and found Elisha son of Shaphat. He was plowing with twelve yoke of oxen, and he himself was driving the twelfth pair. Elijah went up to him and threw his cloak around him. Elisha then left his oxen and ran after Elijah. "Let me kiss my father and mother goodbye," he said, "and then I will come with you."

"Go back," Elijah replied. "What have I done to you?"

So Elisha left him and went back. He took his yoke of oxen and slaughtered them. He burned the plowing equipment to cook the

*meat and gave it to the people, and they ate. Then he set out to fol-
low Elijah and became his servant.*

When Elijah threw his cloak onto Elisha, he was offering to mentor and disciple the young man in service to God. Elisha had a heart
and desire to follow God, so he said goodbye to his family and become
devoted to helping Elijah.

Notice it said he slaughtered his oxen and burned his plow. Elisha
left everything behind and followed Elijah and God wholeheartedly.
He left his old life behind him. He didn't hold on to anything from his
past. He started completely over.

This is excellent example to all the younger men out there who are
just starting out in life. It is important for you to completely destroy
all the sin and behavior in your past and start living differently. As a
believer, we need to follow the Bible's command to leave the old things
behind and become a new creature in Christ. Old habits, sins, desires,
and baggage from our past must be faced and dealt with so you can
enjoy your new life in Christ. Elisha left everything behind and began
a new life serving God.

Over the next few years, we read nothing of Elisha. However, 1
Kings does tell us of numerous times Elijah faced off against Ahab,
trying to turn the wicked king's heart toward God.

We don't hear about Elisha again until 2 Kings chapter 2. This is
the passage I want us to focus on as we study the two men at different
stages in life. For the sake of time, I will just tell you the story. If you
don't want to take my word for it, the story is found in 2 Kings 2. We
will see how their legacy applies first to the younger men.

Elisha and Elijah formed a deep bond over the years. They basically became spiritual father and son. During his prayer time, God
told Elijah that his years of faithful hard work for him were going to
be rewarded. God was going to bring Elijah to heaven in a whirlwind.

Elijah was to travel to the Jordan River. He turned to Elisha and told him to stay in Gilgal. Maybe he didn't want to have to say goodbye to his dear friend. Maybe he didn't want Elisha to have to face the pain of loss. Whatever, the reason, Elijah didn't want Elisha to come along with him. So he asked him to stay behind. However, Elisha would have none of it.

But Elisha said, "As surely as the LORD lives and as you live, I will not leave you." So they went down to Bethel.

Elisha was not leaving Elijah! Even when some prophets came and told Elisha what was going to happen to Elijah, he was not to be deterred. So they travelled toward the Jordan.

Each time they came to a city, Elijah told Elisha to stay there, and he refused. The prophets tried to talk him into staying, but each time Elisha pushed forward.

Eventually, they came to the Jordan River. When they got there, Elijah once again told Elisha to stay there while he crossed over. Let's pick up the story in 2 Kings 2:6

And he [Elisha] replied, "As surely as the LORD lives and as you live, I will not leave you." So the two of them walked on.

Fifty men from the company of the prophets went and stood at a distance, facing the place where Elijah and Elisha had stopped at the Jordan. Elijah took his cloak, rolled it up and struck the water with it. The water divided to the right and to the left, and the two of them crossed over on dry ground.

When they had crossed, Elijah said to Elisha, "Tell me, what can I do for you before I am taken from you?"

Elisha was going to follow his good friend all the way to the end. Nothing or no one was going to separate them. We are now at the part of the story I want to focus on: Two men at two different places in life demonstrate two different paths that all men can relate to and learn from. Let's look first at the lessons for the Elishas in the world.

The Elishas are the younger men who are looking for men to model themselves after. They are desperately searching for men to guide them and be an example to them of how a Christian man should live.

Our churches are full of Elishas. So many boys have single moms raising them, and even though they do the absolute best they can, they can't be both mother and father. We have a generation of Elishas (or if you prefer, Bobs) who need an Elijah to mentor them. Elisha found a model of a godly man in his life, and we see by his response to Elijah's question that he wanted to be just like Elijah.

> **WE HAVE A GENERATION OF ELISHAS WHO NEED AN ELIJAH TO MENTOR THEM!**

When they had crossed, Elijah said to Elisha, "Tell me, what can I do for you before I am taken from you?"

"Let me inherit a double portion of your spirit," Elisha replied.

Elisha was so impressed with what he saw in Elijah that he wanted to be as great a man of God as his mentor. As a matter of fact, he wanted to be twice the man Elijah was. This was the ultimate sign of respect for Elijah, and it is the attitude we all need to have.

Think about it—how many times have you heard it said, "I wish I could be half the man so and so is?" This is meant to be a compliment, and in a way it is, but I believe Elisha has a better perspective. He wanted everything Elijah had and even more of God.

As mentioned earlier, my mom passed away a few years back. My mom was a spiritual pillar in my life. I had a horrible example of what it means to be a godly man in my dad, but I saw godliness modeled in my mom every single day.

My mom taught me so many things, and she made sure her kids grew up in a safe and protected environment. She was strict with her rules and what she allowed us to do and not to do. She had strong beliefs, and she lived them out each and every day. From her, I learned how to pray, how to study the Bible, how to love, how to forgive, how to be honest and trustworthy, and how to develop a deep, intimate relationship with God, just to name a few things. I am eternally grateful for the many things she demonstrated daily.

My mom suffered greatly for her love for God. She endured constant persecution from her husband for her faith in God. Close friends and family turned on her and abandoned her because she fell in love with God wholeheartedly. If, after her death, I had prayed to be half the person she was, Kathy Holden would have come back and smacked me up-side the head and said, "I didn't go through all the pain and torture I went through for you to be half the person I am. I want you to surpass me in God's kingdom!"

I was heart-broken and devastated the night she passed away, but as I lay in bed that night sobbing, I remembered this verse in 2 Kings. Not being one to go part way, I asked God to place four times the power he had on my mom's life onto mine. Kathy Holden's life was not in vain. Her path and legacy lives on in me and in my sister, and our chief purpose in life is to become even greater Christians than she was.

This needs to be the motivation of all believers. We need to find people we can admire, learn all we can from them, and make it our mission in life to continue their legacy by surpassing them in the kingdom. Elisha asked this of Elijah, and as we read Elijah's response, we see the mission for all the Elijahs of the world.

"You have asked a difficult thing," Elijah said, "yet if you see me when I am taken from you, it will be yours—otherwise, it will not."

Notice Elijah did not get offended. He didn't think, "Who does this young twit think he is? Does he think he is better than me?" No; instead, he encourages Elijah to look at him. This needs to be the attitude of all men.

I have a friend and mentor named Tom. Tom is like Elijah. While a lot of leaders would try and keep younger men below them and "in their place," Tom allows us to try our wings and grow. He mentors us and allows us to try things and make a difference. He celebrates our victories with us. I am blessed to have a friend like him who is secure enough to encourage me and other future leaders to go for it with all we've got.

> **IF YOU MULTIPLY TWO TIMES ZERO, YOU GET ZERO. WE CANNOT CONTINUE BEING ZEROES IN GOD'S KINGDOM. WE NEED TO GIVE YOUNGER MEN SOMETHING TO MULTIPLY FROM.**

Men, we need to give the younger men around us an example to model. When Tom Green, the former AG National Men's Director and the speaker at the convention, mentioned the double-portion topic, he said something I never thought of before. He said, "I was never good at math in school, but I do know this: if you multiply two times zero, you get zero."

This is so true. We need to give younger men something to multiply from. We cannot continue being zeroes in God's kingdom. We must live strong, solid lives before God. We must dive into God and build relationships they can learn from and model.

The world is full of compromising and halfhearted models for them to follow. We need to pursue God and give them something to shoot for in their lives. Elijah told Elisha to watch him. It took work and effort on Elisha's part, but he wanted to become a amazing man of God and he strove for it in his life.

> *As they were walking along and talking together, suddenly a chariot of fire and horses of fire appeared and separated the two of them, and Elijah went up to heaven in a whirlwind. Elisha saw this and cried out, "My father! My father! The chariots and horsemen of Israel!" And Elisha saw him no more. Then he took hold of his garment and tore it in two.*

> *Elisha then picked up Elijah's cloak that had fallen from him and went back and stood on the bank of the Jordan. He took the cloak that had fallen from Elijah and struck the water with it. "Where now is the LORD, the God of Elijah?" he asked. When he struck the water, it divided to the right and to the left, and he crossed over.*

> *The company of the prophets from Jericho, who were watching, said, "The spirit of Elijah is resting on Elisha."*

Elisha watched Elijah, and when Elijah was taken away, he received the blessing of God on his life. Everyone around him recognized it immediately. Elijah's godly legacy lived on and increased in Elisha's life. Elisha went on to do an even more powerful work for God than Elijah had done. Guys, this needs to be our aim as well.

Where are you in life?

Are you the young Elisha, yearning for a godly model to follow and emulate in your life?

If so, I encourage you to ask God to bring such a man into your life. When he does, watch him closely. Examine his life, his behavior, his relationships, everything about him. Tell God you respect this man and you want to become twice the man he is. Glean all the knowledge you can from this man and learn from his strengths while avoiding his weaknesses.

Maybe you are an Elijah, an older man living your walk with God. I exhort you today, live a life that gives the younger generation something to build on. Don't become intimidated when the younger men surpass you. Instead, encourage them in their walk with God and continue following God wholeheartedly.

To be honest, many of us are both Elijah and Elisha. We need to be men who glean from those who have gone before us, but also be conscious that there are those younger who are watching us to see what they can glean from us. While we become a "four" to our predecessors' "two," these younger men are trying to become "eights." We must continue our growth for their sakes, giving them godly examples to follow.

Men, we are all in this together. When we all work together to become godly men, we will all grow, and the kingdom of God grows stronger and stronger, dealing a deathblow to our enemy. Generational iniquities will be conquered, sin patterns will be destroyed, and men will walk in freedom! So I encourage you, learn from the examples of Elijah and Elisha. Pursue the double portion of God's Spirit. Embrace mentorship! Together we can do it.

Dear heavenly Father, thank you for this amazing example of what it means to mentor men. Help me as I pursue an Elijah relationship with an older man. Help me learn from his example and to run the race as fast as I can to not only emulate his example, but surpass him in God's kingdom.

Father, I also ask you as you use me as an Elijah to the younger generation so that I live a life that gives them a model to strive after. Help me stay humble and gracious and to help them along the way so that my ceiling is their floor. Help them surpass me in your kingdom and to celebrate with them as they do. In Jesus' name, amen.

LEGACY CHALLENGES

1. Daily pray that God leads you to an Elijah to mentor and disciple you. Also ask God to help you to become a mentor to an Elisha.

2. Honestly ask yourself, "What would be my response if a man I am mentoring surpassed me spiritually?" Take this answer to God and ask him to help you to encourage them to go further than you can go.

EXTREME LEGACY CHALLENGES

Find an activity at your church, like being a youth worker or a Royal Rangers leader, and start investing in the lives of the younger men in your church, especially the ones who don't have a dad in their lives. Go beyond just working at church and make it a part of your everyday life, being a spiritual father to all boys/teens.

GROUP STUDY QUESTIONS

1. Why did Elisha not want to leave Elijah? What was the cause of his devotion?

2. What do you make of Elijah's response to Elisha's request?

3. Are you more like Elijah, Elisha, or are you like both?

4. Is there an Elijah in your life you can model yourself after? How do you plan to do it?

5. Two times zero is still zero. What are some steps to take to make sure we aren't zeroes?

6. Are you secure enough to be Elijah and help the next generation grow?

12

THE AQUILA LEGACY

LEARNING TO SUPPORT
YOUR WIFE

Do you remember your first crush? You know, the girl you were convinced was the perfect girl for you, the one you were destined to marry? My teenage crush was on a Christian singer. I was convinced that God was going to have me marry her! Anyone who knew me at that time of my life knew this.

In my eyes she was the perfect woman. I found her to be one of the most attractive women I had ever seen. She was talented, she had a great personality in her interviews, she had an incredible heart for God, and she loved and served him wholeheartedly. She was a talented singer and an incredible speaker. I was sure we would meet, get married, and conquer the world for God as I preached and she sang. We would truly live happily ever after as we ministered and loved God and each other.

Obviously, it was not meant to be! However, I do still want to get married one day. When I think about the kind of woman I want to marry, the character qualities I listed above are still the same. The idea of who I will marry has changed, but not the dream. I still dream about meeting the woman that God has set aside just for me and I look forward to raising a family together. I also look forward to walking together through life, ministering together, growing together, and serving God together in whatever way he has for us.

This isn't exactly the situation in which I grew up. You see, I grew up with a mother who had the same desires. She longed to minister with her husband. She longed to walk with him in spiritual unity. She wanted pretty much what I mentioned above. However, what she ended up with was a man who turned away from God, his family, and despised any thought of ministry. She lived a life where her dreams were stifled and her desires weren't supported.

As a result, I have learned that it is important for a godly man to support his wife's visions and dreams. I want to someday walk hand-in-hand with my future spouse as we go through life serving God.

There is a man in the Bible who has an awesome legacy as a man who served God side by side with his wife. He never stymied his wife or tried to keep her in her place as she served God. He didn't kill her dreams. Instead, we see a couple who, every time they are mentioned, are mentioned working together, ministering together, loving and supporting each other as they serve their Lord and Master. Who is this man? His name is Aquila.

Before we begin to examine the life of Aquila, I want to take a minute and speak to the single men who are reading this book. You may be tempted to skip over this chapter, thinking it has no relevance to you. I want to encourage you to continue reading this chapter. It is never too soon to begin learning how to be a godly husband. I am writing this chapter as a single man. However, I have realized I do not want to have a repeat performance of the marriage that my parents had, and in order to end up with a different result, I have made it a priority to read and study everything I can about how to be a godly husband. That way, when God leads me to my wife, I can start out fresh with a clear understanding of what it takes to be a godly husband.

Besides, the information in this chapter can be applied to any relationships with women you may have. So I want to encourage you to read on and to even read the recommended reading at the end of the chapter so you too will be prepared to be a godly husband when the time comes. Now, let's get started with our look at Aquila's legacy.

AQUILA ISN'T JUST SOMETHING YOU USE TO WRITE

Go ahead and boo that subtitle, I deserve it! Aquila isn't a name with which many people are familiar. I have personally never met anyone named Aquila. However, such a man did exist in the Bible. Let's turn to Acts 18, which is the first place we read about this man and his awesome legacy.

> After this, Paul left Athens and went to Corinth. There he met a Jew named Aquila, a native of Pontus, who had recently come from Italy with his wife Priscilla, because Claudius had ordered all Jews to leave Rome. Paul went to see them, and because he was a tentmaker as they were, he stayed and worked with them.

Paul liked to support himself financially when he went on his missionary journeys so as not to be a financial burden on the churches that he was visiting. We read here that Paul, besides being a great theologian, a former Pharisee, and now a preacher of the gospel, was also a tentmaker. Upon entering the city, he would have naturally sought out a local tentmaker in hopes of some part-time work. I am sure that Paul was thrilled to not only find work, but to find it working for fellow believers.

We learn a lot about Aquila and his wife Priscilla in this passage. We read that they had recently moved to Corinth from Rome. Due to a rebellious uprising in the city, Claudius banned all Jews from living in Rome. This meant that Aquila and Priscilla were forced to leave Italy, their business, and all that was normal to them. While this would be a terrible strain to most marriages and maybe even the end to some, it appears that their love and devotion to each other only increased.

Once in Corinth, Aquila and Priscilla set up their tent-making shop together. This brings us to the first thing that I want to point out to you as the marks of a godly man. **When opposition and turbulent times came, Aquila took the steps necessary to ensure that the strength of his marriage stayed the same by working with his wife.**

> **WHEN OPPOSITION AND TURBULENT TIMES CAME, AQUILA TOOK THE NECESSARY STEPS TO ENSURE THAT THE STRENGTH OF HIS MARRIAGE STAYED THE SAME BY WORKING WITH HIS WIFE.**

Such a time of turmoil can be extremely devastating for a woman. Women like to feel a sense of security. We read here that any sense of security Priscilla may have felt in Rome was destroyed. Having to start over, we see that Aquila had apparently stepped up to the plate, found them a place to live in Corinth, and established the family business. He took action to ensure the security of his wife. Not only that, but when he started the new business, he made her a part of it. I feel that this is the action of a godly husband. Let me explain why.

Growing up, my father was a very controlling man. He allowed no one to touch the family money or even know how much he made or on what it was spent. There was no family budget in which we all participated.

As a result, my mother lived in a great deal of financial insecurity. She was always fearful of losing our home or going broke. Many years later, we came to find that my father had mishandled a great amount of money and had deceitfully hidden this fact. We were in great financial danger. My mom was devastated.

On top of all this, my father didn't respond well to us finding out the trouble he had gotten into and refused to participate in solving the problem. As a result, my mom was forced to take over the finances, and with my sister's and my help, work our way out of the mess. However, the three of us lost any shred of security we had ever felt.

This is why I think the action taken by Aquila when faced with the tremendous upheaval caused by Claudius was so wonderful. He didn't lay back and do nothing. He didn't leave it to his wife and make her deal with it. Instead, he worked with his wife, and together they moved on and started over. That is the mark of a strong marriage: When faced with tremendous problems, the husband and wife work together to solve the problem and, in the end, become even closer.

Maybe you have faced a devastating loss in your life. It is inevitable that some time in your married life some form of disaster will come. However, a godly man will step up and ensure that his family is taken care of; he will work with his wife as they move forward, and he will make sure that they grow closer and stronger as a result.

Besides being willing to work with his wife, we read that Aquila ministered alongside of his wife. In my opinion, this is the second reason that Aquila was a great man.

Every time we read in the Bible of Aquila, his wife Priscilla is mentioned. They were a joint team. They are never mentioned separately. I love that. Aquila loved his wife, and together they were an unstoppable ministry machine. Let's look together at some of the ministry they undertook together.

The first time we read of this dynamic duo is in Acts 18:3.

Paul went to see them, and because he was a tentmaker as they were, he stayed and worked with them.

We read here that Aquila and his wife not only hired Paul, but they let him stay with them. You may not think this is such a big deal to have a house guest. However, do you know how long Paul stayed with them? The answer is found in verse 11.

So Paul stayed in Corinth for a year and a half, teaching them the word of God.

Yes, you read that right. Paul moved in with them for a year and a half. Not only, that, but if you read the passage, you see that Paul was joined by Timothy and Silas. I am sure that many couples would gladly let the local evangelist stay with them for a day or two, but would you let them and their entire team stay for a year and a half? Most wouldn't, but these two saw it as a ministry and did it together.

The second example we see of them ministering together is seen in Acts 18:24. When we rejoin Aquila and Priscilla, we see that they have once again moved, this time from Corinth to Ephesus.

Meanwhile a Jew named Apollos, a native of Alexandria, came to Ephesus. He was a learned man, with a thorough knowledge of the Scriptures. He had been instructed in the way of the Lord, and he spoke with great fervor and taught about Jesus accurately, though he knew only the baptism of John. He began to speak boldly in the synagogue. When Priscilla and Aquila heard him, they invited him to their home and explained to him the way of God more adequately.

We read here that while living in Ephesus, Aquila and Priscilla came across a revival meeting being led by an elegant young speaker named Apollos. After listening to him, they were impressed by the power and conviction with which he spoke. However, they immediately recognized that while his heart was in the right place, his theology wasn't complete.

Seeing his tender heart and desire to know and serve God, Aquila and his wife took Apollos aside and taught him the true gospel of salvation. As a result, he learned the true gospel and became one of the greatest preachers that the early church had ever heard, leading multitudes to Christ. He was known far and wide as an amazing speaker, way better than Paul. All this was made possible because of these dynamic ministering spouses.

The third area we read that Aquila and Priscilla ministered together is seen in Romans 16:3–5:

Greet Priscilla and Aquila, my co-workers in Christ Jesus. They risked their lives for me. Not only I but all the churches of the Gentiles are grateful to them. Greet also the church that meets at their house.

Paul also references that Aquila and Priscilla had started a church in their house in 1 Corinthians 16:19. Apparently, after having lived in Corinth and Ephesus, the two had decided to move back to their original home in Rome. Once there, they began witnessing to the Romans which led to them starting a church in their home.

These two were able to take the gospel message to what was then the heart of modern civilization. It is amazing what can happen when a husband and wife minister together as equal partners!

What about you? Are you willing to minister side by side with your wife? Do you have the same heart for God and ministry that your wife possesses? Ministry together should always be the result when a godly man walks side by side with his wife in unity together.

The final aspect to study as to what made Aquila a godly man is seen in the verse mentioned above from Romans 16. Take a second and read it carefully. Do you notice anything odd about it? It's there to be seen, but until I researched and studied for this chapter I never saw it. What is it? Notice the placement of the names. It lists Priscilla's name before Aquila's.

This probably seems like no big deal to you. I mean, we live in a culture where we supposedly hold to the theory, "Ladies before Gentlemen."

However, this is not the way things were in the days of Aquila. In his time, people were listed in order of importance and stature. Take for example the list of Jesus' disciples listed in the Gospels. Each listed the disciples in order of prominence in the group, beginning with Peter, the leader.

It is especially odd to find a woman's name listed first in those days. So why exactly is she listed first both here and in other passages?

The answer seems to be that she was the more prominent of the two in the early church, implying that she was the more effective minister.

I find this fascinating. How many men would be willing to not only minister side by side with their wives, but also be willing to have her receive the praise and be given credit for being more effective than he?

> **A GODLY MAN WILL ENCOURAGE HIS WIFE TO BECOME ALL SHE CAN BE, AND WILL DO ALL THAT HE CAN TO HELP HER REACH HER GOAL.**

I know that in my younger days I would have been intimidated to death and probably would have tried to squelch her and build myself up. How do I know this? Because this is what I grew up seeing my father do to my mother.

My mom was an incredible woman. She was of the strongest Christians I know. Every fiber of her being was geared to loving, obeying, and serving God. She was a woman who loved to dream big. However, my father was the exact opposite. He tolerated God in our family. He went to church on Sundays, but that was about it.

He never sought to read or study the Bible and I don't think he prayed. He just wanted to be thought of as a great Christian.

My mom loved to teach other people the ways of God, and she would always try and include my dad. However, he would have none of it. He would find ways to discourage my mom, undermine her abilities, and end any ministry opportunities in which she became involved.

As a result, he destroyed her dreams and made her feel that God would never let her minister for him again. All of this because my dad couldn't accept that my mom was a strong, growing Christian. Instead of challenging himself and trying to grow spiritually, he would tear her down so he wouldn't have to grow.

Thankfully, God did a tremendous heart-healing inside my mom and helped her work through the lies and the pain caused by my dad, but this should never have been. A godly man will encourage his wife to become all that she can be, and will do all that he can to help her reach that goal. He should admire her and seek ways to increase himself to grow alongside of her. He should try and help her fulfill her dreams. He should praise her and build her up. Her success should be his greatest joy.

This is a lesson I had to learn before God allowed me to begin full-time ministry. I know what you're thinking, "Jamie, you're single, where are you going with this?"

Yes, I am single, but I work with women on a daily basis. Years ago, God put me through this school of encouraging and supporting women. With my background, it wasn't my nature at all. But God loves to take our sinful nature and turn it into a godly legacy, and he set out to do this in me.

I went through a season of time where I was not allowed to minister. Instead, I supported my older sister, Adessa, as she ministered. I carried her bags as an assistant. I spent countless hours sitting behind her ministry table while she spoke at events. I chauffeured her from place to place as she fulfilled her calling. I will not lie to you and say it was easy. It was *so* hard for me as I thought things like, "When is it my turn?" or, "I should be speaking, not selling t-shirts and CDs." Just keeping it real here, guys.

But this season was so incredibly necessary in my life as I learned the lessons that Aquila thrived at. Before God ever gave me the privilege of running Mantour Ministries, I learned to take a back seat and let others shine. I learned to encourage and support women in ministry and in life, not follow the generational pattern of "keeping women in their place." Now I work in partnership with my sister all the time on men's and women's ministry, as I encourage her to go for whatever dream God lays on her heart. She knows I am her biggest fan and she has my total support.

This is what I believe was the attitude of Aquila, and it should be the attitude of any man who wants to have the legacy of a godly husband.

Why do we need to make this our attitude? Because failing to do so is a direct sin against God. Let's look at Ephesians 5:25.

Husbands, love your wives, just as Christ loved the church and gave himself up for her.

We are commanded here by the apostle Paul to love our wives like Jesus loved the church. We see Jesus providing a sense of security for his church in that we have eternal security, that we will have eternal life in heaven with him. He did this by laying down his life for us. In the same way, God's men must give their wives the same sense of protection and security here on earth by laying down their lives for them.

We know that Jesus has given us a helper, the Holy Spirit, who is ready and willing to work side by side with us in whatever we do in life, especially when we minister. In the same way, a godly man should be willing to work with his wife, side by side, and be her helper.

Finally, we know that Jesus' main desire is for us to grow spiritually and to become strong, mature, godly Christians. He is thrilled when we succeed. He loves to help us fulfill godly dreams and aspirations. Likewise, a godly man should have the same attitude in his relationship with his wife. He should delight in her success. He should commit himself to helping her achieve her dreams. Her growth and success should be his greatest joy. Then, like Aquila, you can be a great man who is committed to being the best and most godly husband you can be.

Remember: Aquila had Paul living with him for a year and a half. He knew this teaching of Paul, and I believe the evidence is there that he obeyed.

While these three areas we discussed aren't the only ingredients to a successful marriage, they are good foundations on which to begin and grow. So I encourage you to, like Aquila, step up to the plate and develop a legacy as a supportive, godly husband. God demands it and your wife deserves nothing less.

Dear heavenly Father, thank you for giving this wonderful woman to me to spend the rest of my life with her. Forgive me for not always being the godly husband she has needed for me to be. From this day forward, I want to commit myself to become the godly husband that you want me to be. Show me ways that I can provide security for my wife. Open doors of ministry for us to do together. Help me to always lift up and encourage my wife. Don't allow me to ever become intimidated by her successes, but to instead rejoice in them and become inspired by them. I love my wife, and I want to be all that she needs me to be. Help me in this pursuit. In Jesus' name, amen.

LEGACY CHALLENGE

1. Ask your wife if she feels secure about life with you. Honestly listen and make any necessary changes.

2. Sit down with your wife and discuss with her any dreams or visions she has that she wants to fulfill. Then think of ways you can encourage her or help her accomplish her dreams.

3. Read the book *Every Man's Marriage* by Fred Stoeker.

EXTREME LEGACY CHALLENGES

Volunteer to do some form of service together at your church. Some ideas: Lead a Sunday school class, prepare a meal for an event at church, clean the church together, etc. Be creative, but make sure you serve together as a team.

GROUP STUDY QUESTIONS

1. We discussed the need your wife has for security and how it is your job to ensure her security. Discuss this and different ways it can be accomplished.

2. How well do you work with your wife? What are some steps you can take to work better together?

3. How do you react in times of crisis? Is this beneficial or harmful to your wife's sense of security?

4. Do you and your wife ever minister together? What are some ways you can do this?

5. Do you encourage your wife to become all that she can be, and do you do all that you can to help her reach her goals?

6. How often do you praise and build up your wife?

7. Is your wife's success a source of joy to you or does it make you feel inferior? Why?

8. How does the way that Jesus treated the church relate to how you should treat your wife?

13

THE ONESIPHORUS LEGACY

BEING A LOYAL MAN

Most of my life I have been a huge fan of the Denver Broncos. I was loyal to the Broncos through the good times and the bad. I was a fan during each of their three Super Bowl losses in the '80s. I was faithful to them through all the years when they didn't make it to the Super Bowl. I was loyal to the Broncos famed quarterback John Elway, even when it appeared he would never win a Super Bowl. (This bond was tested a few years back when he traded away Tebow, but I worked through my feelings). I suffered through the smackdown Seattle's Legion of Boom gave to Peyton Manning and the gang in Super Bowl XLVIII. For years, I endured all the jokes and ridicule as I stayed loyal to the orange and blue.

Then it happened! In 1998, when I was a junior in college, John Elway and the Broncos made it to the Super Bowl! They were facing the defending World Champion Green Bay Packers, and NO ONE gave them a chance. I was excited, nervous, scared, and joyful all at the same time. Everyone knew this was John Elway's last chance to win a

Super Bowl. I remember I went to church that day in my #7 jersey and wore it all day long.

Finally, the kickoff came. The game turned out to be a real battle, culminating with the Broncos taking the lead with, if I remember correctly, less than two minutes remaining. The entire world watched to see if John Elway would finally win his first Super Bowl. It all hinged on the Packer's final drive!

The Packers drove past midfield, but were stopped on the first three downs. The game came down to fourth and ten. Brett Favre dropped back and delivered a rifle pass across the middle of the field.

My heart stopped beating as the ball soared through the air. Suddenly the Broncos linebacker leaped up and batted the ball down, securing the Super Bowl win!!

To say I was thrilled was an understatement. I went crazy just like any avid fan would do! Finally, the Broncos had won the Super Bowl and all my years of heartbreaking loyalty were rewarded. The icing on the cake came the following year when John Elway returned for a final season and defended his title, winning back-to-back Super Bowls. All the years of ridicule and laughter I endured as a Broncos fan were over, and my loyalty as a fan grew deeper.

This is a common experience for all sports fans. Through the good times and the bad, the highs and the lows, we continue to give our support and loyalty to our team.

Unfortunately, in the culture in which we live, it seems that men will support a team full of men they have never met, but not their fellow brothers in need. I wonder how many men show the same amount of loyalty to their fellow brothers in Christ?

When hard times come, are we there to lift our brothers up, to support them, to cheer them on, and to help them in whatever way possible?

I believe it is time that we as men begin to show loyalty to our fellow brothers. We need to get to the place where we build each other up and help carry each other in the tough times. Buried in the book of 2 Timothy, we read of a man named Onesiphorus. He is an excellent example to us of how to be a loyal man. He had a legacy of being loyal even when it was costly to him.

Onesiphorus is not one of the better-known men in the Bible, but his story touches the heart. His mention in the annals of history is small, a total of four verses in the Bible. However, he appears at a crucial point in the life of one of the most well-known biblical heroes, the apostle Paul.

Second Timothy is a heart-wrenching letter, written by Paul to his spiritual son, Timothy. He wrote this letter while he was a prisoner in a Roman dungeon. When you read this letter, you can sense the raw emotion Paul is feeling. He is well aware that his pending execution could come at any moment. He wants to leave one last letter for his beloved Timothy to let him know how his last days were spent. He sought to strengthen and encourage the young man who would soon be forced to minister without his influence. It is in this context that we read of Onesiphorus. Let's look at the first verse of the passage together.

You know that everyone in the province of Asia has deserted me, including Phygelus and Hermogenes (I Timothy 1:15).

Paul was being held prisoner in the city of Rome because he served Jesus. The Roman government considered their emperor to be god. This particular emperor was Nero, a man known throughout history as being insane, and he saw the apostle Paul as a traitor. Because of Paul's preaching, Nero had him arrested and sentenced to death.

While he was in prison, we read in verse 15 that all of the people Paul trusted deserted him because they were fearful of execution. Among the deserters are two men named Phygelus and Hermogenes.

It isn't clear who these two men are in this passage. We do know they were two men Paul trusted. Apparently, it was unthinkable that they, of all people, would desert him, because they are the only two deserters mentioned by name.

They were friends, maybe even fellow leaders in the church, but they deserted Paul when he needed them most. These men had no sense of loyalty. They cared more about their personal safety and comfort than they cared about supporting and encouraging Paul. Such disloyalty is a disgrace for any man who claims to be a godly man. It is the makings of a coward, not a man.

A man who wants to become like Jesus will not act this way. He will support and help a friend no matter what he is facing. Onesiphorus was such a man.

The first mention of Onesiphorus is seen in the three verses following the heartbreaking revelation from Paul that all the people he was relying on had deserted him. Let's look at 2 Timothy 1:16–18.

May the Lord show mercy to the household of Onesiphorus, because he often refreshed me and was not ashamed of my chains. On the contrary, when he was in Rome, he searched hard for me until he found me. May the Lord grant that he will find mercy from the Lord on that day! You know very well in how many ways he helped me in Ephesus.

Onesiphorus traveled hundreds of miles to the city of Rome to see his good friend Paul. When he arrived in Rome, he searched zealously for Paul. This was no quiet, secretive search in hopes of not being discovered, but a tenacious, vigorous search. He must have gone door to door and store to store, asking anyone and everyone where he could find Paul. He had no fear or shame at being associated with Paul. All he knew was that his friend needed help, and he was going to do all he could to find him and help him.

Today, this may not seem like a big deal. If I had a friend who was in prison, I could go to the jail and visit him without suffering any personal consequences. However, this was not the case in Paul's time.

In those days, if you went to visit a prisoner, you were regarded as a criminal or worse. This was especially true if you visited a prisoner like Paul who was scheduled to be executed. You would be considered a traitor to the Roman Empire, putting your own life in great danger.

This is why it is even more impressive to read that Onesiphorus searched so intently for Paul. He didn't care if he was viewed as a criminal or a traitor. He felt no shame that the man he was searching for was in chains in a Roman dungeon. All he cared about was being loyal to his friend in his time of need.

Can you imagine the boost that Onesiphorus' visit must have given to a very discouraged Paul?

Face it, Paul was human. Being deserted by all these believers had to have some effect on his spirit. However, he must have been overjoyed by this visit from his loyal friend.

Stop and think about it. How much did Onesiphorus' visit shape the content of Paul's second epistle to Timothy?

- Would he have been so bold in telling Timothy to never be ashamed of the gospel if he hadn't witnessed Onesiphorus' lack of shame in searching him out?
- Could he have commanded Timothy in chapter 4 to preach the Word with boldness if he wasn't positive that God would supply Timothy with his own Onesiphorus in his time of need?

Who knows what difference there would be in Paul's final letter to Timothy. Thankfully, we don't have to wonder because of the shining legacy of loyalty from Onesiphorus.

We live in a world that needs more men like Onesiphorus. Loyalty is a rare commodity. We have lots of men like Phygelus and Hermogenes. The world is full of wimps who refuse to be loyal to those around them.

How do I know this? I have been one of them.

I want to take this time to get real with you about this subject of loyalty. I don't want you to feel that I am arrogantly pointing my finger at you as I say that we as men don't have a good sense of loyalty. I want you to know that this chapter is directed at me just as much, if not more, than at you.

In my past, I have struggled with not being loyal to the people God has placed in my life. For me, it is a source of great shame and disgrace. Let me give you an example.

When I was in high school, I had a best friend. We did everything together. We spent hours talking, hanging out, listening to music, basically just being friends. We went to the same school and the same church. We enjoyed many of the same things. However, as I graduated high school and prepared for college, our friendship drastically changed.

One reason for the change was that he began to date a girl. Because of my own insecurities, I became jealous. I was never popular with girls, and I was jealous that he had a girlfriend and I didn't.

Naturally, he spent more time with her and less with me. Still struggling with the emotional pain from my father's rejection, I felt rejected once again. (This was a recurring theme in most of my younger friendships. I perceived rejection that wasn't there because I never faced the pain of the rejection from my father.) As a result, I pulled back. When it was time to go to college, I ended the friendship by not staying in contact. I didn't see or talk to my friend until a few years later.

During my sophomore year of college, I became extremely ill. I ended up in the hospital. It was so serious that my doctors thought I was going to die. However, God miraculously healed me and I made a full recovery.

When my friend heard that I was so sick, he rushed to see me. However, instead of rebuilding our friendship, I became embarrassed and stand-offish. As a result, we were never close again. Occasionally, I see him, but it is awkward.

Looking back now, I deeply regret the way I acted in this friendship. I missed attending his wedding. I missed the birth of his first child, a little girl. There are still times that I miss my friend. However, because of my lack of loyalty, I ruined a great friendship.

My lack of loyalty has been a major source of pain both to myself and those around me. It has cost me good friendships. It almost cost me my relationship with my family, especially my mom.

However, one day God grabbed me and forced me to look at this problem in my life. He showed me how wrong it is that I can be so die-hard-loyal to something as trivial as a football team, yet have no sense of loyalty to the people he had placed in my life. He told me that if I didn't face this and change, I would never be the man he wants me to be.

He confronted me that I would never be a good husband and my marriage would end in divorce the first time I felt my wife hurt me. He said I could never be an effective minister because I would cut people off instead of reaching out to help them. I would not be an Onesiphorus.

In shame and disgrace, I was forced to face this issue and begin to learn what it was that caused me to be so disloyal. God showed me that my lack of loyalty was a direct result of the rejection I felt from my father. In order to never again face the pain of rejection, I pulled away from people so they couldn't hurt me. This defensive act of pulling away is what caused my lack of loyalty.

In order to start being loyal to people, I had to face this pain and realize that not everyone will reject me like my dad. I needed to become vulnerable with people and open myself up to the possibility of being hurt. The Holy Spirit forced me to face the pain buried in my heart that caused me to run from people.

As a result, God has taught me to be loyal. He rebuilt my relationships with my family. My mother and I redeveloped our relationship before she passed away.

God taught me how to support people and help them through the hard times. I have meaningful, lasting relationships.

The Holy Spirit taught me how to forgive and reach out to people in need. None of this would have been possible without facing my problem with loyalty and identifying the root of my problem.

> **IN ORDER TO BECOME A LOYAL MAN, YOU MUST IDENTIFY WHAT IT IS THAT CAUSES YOUR LACK OF LOYALTY.**

In order to become a loyal man, you must identify what it is that causes your lack of loyalty. Then you can work through it and overcome it. You can be free to be the loyal, supportive man you are destined to become.

I hope you can see why I feel so strongly about this subject. I long to see a Christian community where the men can stand side by side, holding each other up through whatever they face.

I yearn to see men who are loyal to their wives and never even consider the idea of divorce. I want there to be men who are loyal to their children. I want to see men who are able to reach the unsaved, and have the new believer know that Christian men can be trusted to stand by them and not cut and run.

What about you?

Would you be willing to do what Onesiphorus did for a friend?

Are you a man committed to being loyal to those around you?

Are you like I once was, resembling Phygelus and Hermogenes, willing to turn my back on those God had placed around me?

Are you completely loyal when it comes to your marriage?

Does your wife know that no matter what happens or what problems the two of you may face, you are committed to her and the marriage and that divorce is never an option?

Do your kids know that no matter what, you will stay?

I encourage you to examine yourself. Take a good look. Develop a legacy of loyalty like Onesiphorus. Be loyal to those God has given you. Who knows what a difference we could make in the life of the friends and family God has given us! Who knows what our legacy will be!

Dear heavenly Father, I want to become a man who practices loyalty. Thank you for all the people you have placed in my life. Forgive me for not demonstrating loyalty to them, but instead doing what is best for me. Help me to become a loyal man. Show me how, through your Word and prayer, what it is that causes me to be disloyal, and then help me to change. I want to become a loyal man whom you and others can count on, especially in time of need. Thank you for hearing this prayer. In Jesus' name, amen

LEGACY CHALLENGES

Take time alone and examine your relationships. Dissect whether or not you are truly loyal to the people in your life. Do the same with your past relationships. Repent if necessary and take action to change.

EXTREME LEGACY CHALLENGES

Find someone who is going through a rough time. For example, find a man who is undergoing a serious family illness or injury, or find a man who is struggling to deal with pain from his past. If you can't think of anyone, ask your pastor. Then go to this person and give him all the help possible. Stay committed to him and see him through his crisis.

GROUP STUDY QUESTIONS

1. What do you consider a loyal man to be? Do you think you are this way?

2. Have you ever had people desert you in a time of need? Have you ever done this to others?

3. Would you be willing to help and comfort a friend if it endangered your personal safety and comfort?

4. How does loyalty relate to a marriage? If asked, do you think your wife would say you are loyal?

5. We read that Onesiphorus traveled from Ephesus to Rome to see Paul, a trip over hundreds of miles. Would you do the same for a friend in need?

6. What are some ways that you can improve in the area of loyalty?

14

THE MARK LEGACY

LEARNING TO QUIT QUITTING

"My wife is driving me crazy, all we ever do is fight! We started off so well, but now I don't see how we can make this marriage work anymore. The new girl at work treats me like a king; I would be so much happier with a woman like her."

"I can't believe I was passed over for promotion again! I gave my heart and soul to this company, and my work is always unappreciated. I am fed up, I want to quit. Even though I have nothing else lined up, I so want to tell off my boss and storm out. I can't take it anymore!"

"I can't take being a dad anymore! It is always something with these kids. Injuries, whining, they always need something, sometimes I wish I was single again. I don't see how I can stick with this. Maybe I should walk away."

"I am so sick of going to church! It's supposed to be a place for support and edification, but it is just a place full of drama and people backstabbing each other. I am sick of it. I think I will quit going to church and just sleep in on Sundays."

"UGH! I came home again tonight ready to woo my wife and have a night of marital bliss. I have been thinking about it all day and I am ready to go. Now that I am home, she is covered in baby puke and says she is exhausted. Another night of no action; maybe I should just hop online. At least there I can find a happy, attractive woman who isn't covered in puke!"

Okay, for many of us these stories are a bit extreme, but yet, in reality, they aren't. Every day our enemy uses common activities and situations to make us feel frustrated and discouraged. He blows things out of proportion and makes us consider doing things we never thought we would do. Others are facing struggles that are even worse than these. Dealing with things they never thought they'd encounter, they feel discouraged and hopeless.

Whatever the situation, many of us are facing the temptation to turn and walk away from whatever area we are struggling with in life. Unfortunately, our society is being overrun by men who are quitting. Because it's such a serious and relevant topic, we are going to discuss the sin of quitting.

There is a man in the Bible named Mark who struggled with this same tendency to quit and run away. Throughout this chapter, we will see the devastating effects this behavior had on his life and relationships. Also, we will see that God was able to take him and change him into a man who developed a legacy of not quitting, who would stand firm. He became a reliable man. This is encouraging for those of us who need to stop quitting.

As a young person, Mark was privileged to be around Jesus. The Scriptures seem to indicate that he came from a wealthy family. His family used their wealth to support the ministry of Jesus. It may have been their home which contained the upper room used by Jesus for his last supper with the disciples.

The first time we read about Mark in the Bible seems to be in the book bearing his name. Let's take a look at the passage.

A young man, wearing nothing but a linen garment, was following Jesus. When they seized him, he fled naked, leaving his garment behind (Mark 14:51–52).

This event took place when Jesus was arrested and his disciples fled. Since this account is found in the Gospel of Mark, it is believed to be this same Mark.

Apparently, Mark was in bed when he heard Jesus and the disciples leave the upper room. He decided to follow them. When the mob came and arrested Jesus, it is possible they may have tried to seize his followers. This young man was grabbed, but he was able to escape by leaving his blanket and running away naked. This is the first time we read about Mark running away.

It isn't until many years later that we read again about Mark. By this time he has grown into a man and finds himself with the opportunity to minister side by side with one of the greatest missionaries to ever walk the globe, the apostle Paul.

Among the prophets and teachers of the church at Antioch of Syria were Barnabas, Simeon…, Lucius (from Cyrene), Manaen (the childhood companion of King Herod Antipas), and Saul [also called Paul]. *One day as these men were worshiping the Lord and fasting, the Holy Spirit said, "Dedicate Barnabas and Saul for the special work to which I have called them." So after more fasting and prayer, the men laid their hands on them and sent them on their way. So Barnabas and Saul were sent out by the Holy Spirit. They went down to the seaport of Seleucia and then sailed for the island of Cyprus. There, in the town of Salamis, they went to the Jewish synagogues and preached the word of God. John Mark went with them as their assistant* (Acts 13:1–4 NLT).

Paul and Barnabas were handpicked by God to go far and wide and preach the gospel. Mark was sent along as their assistant. Barnabas was Mark's uncle, and he had grown up around Jesus and the disciples. He was the obvious choice for the job. It was the internship that most men can only imagine.

Mark was given the privilege of being the right hand man for the evangelistic dream team. He would serve alongside of them and take care of all their needs. What an opportunity! Unfortunately, as we continue on through the book of Acts, we learn it was an opportunity that Mark squandered.

Paul and his companions then left Paphos by ship for Pamphylia, landing at the port town of Perga. There John Mark left them and returned to Jerusalem (Acts 13:13 NLT).

While the passage seems to simply read that Mark returned home, a deeper meaning is implied. He didn't just return home because he was not needed anymore. He abandoned them. He ran away and left them alone without a younger man to help them.

It is important to realize his job description.

Paul and Barnabas were probably middle-aged men. Everywhere they went, they went on foot. They had to carry their own supplies. They had to protect themselves from animals and thieves. This was probably the reason why a strapping guy like Mark was sent along. He was to be their muscle, their pack horse, their physical support as they did their spiritual work.

When he abandoned them, they were forced to pick up his responsibilities and balance both the spiritual and physical work, bearing the weight and exhaustion that accompanied each set of duties. Fortunately, they met another young man named Timothy who picked up Mark's responsibilities.

What was it that made Mark quit and abandon them? Scripture doesn't say. Maybe he hated the hard labor he was forced to endure.

Maybe he was homesick. Maybe he resented the fact that Paul seemed to become the more dominant leader of the group instead of his uncle Barnabas. Perhaps they ran into trials or persecution. The Bible just doesn't say. All we know is something spooked him, and as a result, he ran home and left the missionary team high and dry.

Eventually, Paul and Barnabas returned from their successful missionary trip and began to plan another journey to check up on the new converts. As the two men began making plans, an argument erupted between them.

> *Barnabas wanted to take John, also called Mark, with them, but Paul did not think it wise to take him, because he had deserted them in Pamphylia and had not continued with them in the work. They had such a sharp disagreement that they parted company. Barnabas took Mark and sailed for Cyprus, but Paul chose Silas and left, commended by the believers to the grace of the Lord* (Acts 15:37–40).

Wow! Can you imagine what it must have felt like to be the cause of the splintering of one of the greatest ministry teams ever to be formed? Talk about feeling humiliated and useless.

Paul was not about to take Mark back out on the road again. Mark had already quit on him once! He was not going through that a second time.

Paul made it perfectly clear that he had no use for Mark as a helper. He was not reliable and couldn't be trusted. How's that for glowing a recommendation to attach to your résumé?

On the other hand, Barnabas had a desire to help Mark and restore him to a place of usefulness for God. He saw Mark's potential and he wanted to help him reach it. As a result, Paul and Barnabas went their separate ways.

GOOD OLD-FASHIONED MATH— TWO IS MORE THAN ONE!

It is important to understand that God allowed these two men to split up because he had different callings for each of them. Now there would be two teams ministering instead of one. Paul chose Silas to go with him to minister to the Gentiles. Barnabas chose Mark to accompany him and they ministered to the Jews.

Barnabas and Mark were relatives. He encouraged Mark and was patient with him. He knew that Mark had to overcome his tendency to quit. Barnabas wouldn't allow Mark's habit of quitting to continue in his life.

He discipled Mark. He made Mark get back up, move forward, and continue to minister. Whenever the sin of quitting rose its ugly head in Mark, Barnabas was there to make him get up, not quit and keep moving forward. What was the result?

Because Barnabas made Mark get back out there and minister, Mark became a man who learned to persevere. He overcame his pattern of quitting. He developed into a strong, dependable, persevering man who could be counted on even when things got tough.

Mark became useful to God. He was restored to a place of ministry. He ministered alongside of Barnabas for years. God used all the trials, new experiences, and people Mark encountered to develop perseverance in him.

Later, Mark worked under Peter. He wrote the Gospel of Mark based on the teachings set out for him by Peter. His relationship with Paul was restored. Read what Paul wrote from jail in his second letter to Timothy:

Only Luke is with me. Get Mark and bring him with you, because he is helpful to me in my ministry.

We know from our discussion of Onesiphorus that visiting someone in prison was a dangerous and degrading assignment, but Paul had a renewed confidence in Mark. He asked him to come and help him.

Mark was able to face the behavioral pattern of quitting, deal with it, and become a man who persevered. He developed a new legacy and became a man that could be counted on and trusted.

I can really relate to Mark. I know quitting was a HUGE pattern in my life. I was the type of person that quit and didn't finish things.

As a child, I quit Little League. I quit guitar and piano lessons. I never finished a painting I started. I began quitting on people and relationships when they failed me or didn't meet my needs. I quit on friends when I didn't feel I measured up to them.

This behavioral pattern started small in me, but it ballooned out of proportion. At one point, I even quit on the promises God had given to me. Let me explain.

About ten years ago, my dad decided to retire from his job. Because he abused me throughout my life, I had a lot of anger and hatred toward him. As a result, I could not stand him being around all the time. I couldn't stand seeing all the ways I was like him.

I began to retreat inside myself. I stopped facing the issues in my life. I became withdrawn and depressed. On top of all this, I went through a severe back injury. The injury forced us to be around each other a lot. It also became the instrument I used to escape the pain in my soul.

Instead of pushing myself and working to get better, I quit.

I was tired of waiting on God to move in my life. I couldn't stand being around my father and having to face how much of him was inside me. I didn't want to keep analyzing myself. I didn't want to keep going through the pain. So I quit.

I stopped moving forward. I stopped trying to get better. Instead, I went with the injury and used it like a crutch. I entered a deep state of depression.

For one year, I rarely left the house. I didn't get dressed. I didn't shave regularly. I gave up. I sat down and buried myself in books, TV, video games, and food.

I convinced myself that I was not sinning. I told myself God would heal my back when it was his time for me to minister. I convinced myself I had faced all my problems and I was okay with God. But I wasn't. I was not moving forward with God.

> **WE, LIKE MARK, CAN FACE THE BEHAVIORAL PATTERN OF QUITTING, DEAL WITH IT, AND BECOME A MAN WHO PERSEVERES.**

As a result, my body got worse. The lack of activity weakened my back even more than the injury. I gained weight because I used M&Ms to ease the hurt in my heart. My people skills got worse because I rarely left the house. I was in serious trouble, all because I quit.

After one year, God used my mom to make me face myself. She spoke facts to me that I didn't want to hear. She told me I was heading toward a wheelchair. I was overweight and out of shape. She said I needed to make changes, major changes.

At first, I was angry at her for being honest and loving me enough to make me look at myself and the trouble I was facing. However, I eventually realized she was right. I had to make drastic changes.

God made me look at my tendency to quit. He showed me it was sin. He showed me that if I wanted to be a new man whose life was dedicated to him, I would have to stop being a quitter and start developing perseverance. Then he put me on an intense discipline schedule to break the pattern of quitting.

The first thing I had to do was face the sin of quitting. I had to realize what caused me to quit and why I gave in to it. I repented of this terrible sin. Next, I had to make huge changes in my life.

I had to deal with the abuse from my father. I finally had to admit that it happened and face the pain of it.

I talked about it.

I remembered things.

I cried and let it all out from inside of me.

I admitted to myself and God that I hated my father and did not want to be around him because I did not want to be abused anymore.

Then I had to learn to live with my father. Fortunately, by this time he had returned to work and my time with him was limited. However, God did arrange situations in which I had to spend time with him. I even had to help him with a physical problem he was experiencing.

It wasn't easy, but God helped me overcome. When I stopped running from the damage done to me by my father's abuse and faced it, I was able to move forward in my life.

Then, I had to force myself to get back into life. I needed to rebuild strength in my back and body. I began a daily exercise program. At first, I could only walk for five minutes at a time because of the extreme pain in my back. However, through lots of pain and hard work, I was able to increase my time more and more.

I disciplined my eating habits. I went on a strict diet. I wrote down everything I ate and began eating more fruits and vegetables and a lot less junk food. I started trying new, healthier foods that I refused to eat before.

I began taking on more chores and responsibilities. I forced myself to go everywhere my family went, no matter how much pain the car caused my back. I began to drive again. It took about a year and a half, but eventually I could function normally and drive anywhere I chose.

I had to fight the sin of quitting. I have experienced the devastation it left on my life, and I never want to go through that again.

I can no longer be a quitter. I must finish what I start. I must be persistent and persevere.

Perseverance is a necessity to becoming a new man who lives a godly life. Paul teaches us in Romans 5:3–4 that if we want to develop character, we need to develop perseverance.

A man with perseverance refuses to quit. He believes God will do what he promised to do. He believes that God is true to his Word. He never stops believing no matter who else doubts, criticizes, mocks, or persecutes him. Quitting is never an option!

This is a very serious topic. If we do not overcome the practice of quitting or running, we could jeopardize our relationship with God and our very salvation.

I believe that if God moves forward and you stop, then you are backsliding. When I started to overcome my year-long depression, one of the first things I had to do was repent of backsliding. Then I began to move forward with God again. A man who longs to become a mature, godly man will always move forward with God and will never quit.

PERSEVERANCE IS A NECESSITY TO BECOMING A GODLY MAN!

I recently attended a men's conference where the speaker, Tommy Barnett, said that he literally tore out the word *quit* from his dictionary. That's commitment to not be a quitter, and it's an excellent example of the passion we need to have to overcome the tendency to quit!

What about you? Are you the type of man who is prone to quitting or running away? Do you have a heart that perseveres no matter what it takes?

What is keeping you from becoming a man who can be counted on and relied upon when things get tough? Do people question whether or not you will be there in a time of need?

These are questions we must face. We must identify what triggers us to run away or quit.

When did it start? Is it a family pattern? Is it a result of hurt and pain caused by another? Is it a tendency you learned from another family member?

Face the cause of this behavioral pattern. Deal with these sins. You can become a persevering man who follows God whatever he asks or whatever the cost. Mark developed a new legacy and so can you!

Dear heavenly Father, please forgive me for every time I have quit or run away. I no longer want to be a man who is a quitter. I want to be a man who develops mature, godly character. I want to become like Jesus. I realize in order for me to do this, I must develop perseverance. I must become a man who persists through whatever I face, knowing that any trials will produce godly character inside of me. I want to become a man of perseverance. Help me stay dedicated to this goal. In Jesus' name, amen.

LEGACY CHALLENGES

Make a list of every time you have ever quit something or have run away from a situation. Analyze what caused this reaction inside of you. Then repent and ask God to forgive you.

Determine to never quit again. Finally, examine the list you made and finish what you quit. This will help you develop perseverance.

EXTREME LEGACY CHALLENGES

Find one thing that you quit in your life and finish it. For example, maybe it's time to finish that project you started on your home and never quite wrapped up. Perhaps you need to take a few classes and finish your degree. Whatever it may be, finish something you quit and turn your failure into a personal victory.

GROUP STUDY QUESTIONS

1. As a child, did you quit a lot of things? Did it carry on into your adult life?

2. Have you ever taken the time to analyze why you quit things? What did you discover?

3. Have you ever quit on God?

4. We mentioned the devastating effects Mark's quitting had on Paul's ministry team. Has your quitting affected other people?

5. What is perseverance? How does is it relate to character development?

6. I made the statement that quitting can lead to backsliding. How does this happen?

7. What can you do to make up for all the times you have quit? What action can you take?

CONCLUSION

―――・◆・―――

SO WHAT? WHAT DOES IT REALLY MATTER IF I DEVELOP A GODLY LEGACY?

We have reached the end of this part of our journey together toward developing a legacy as a godly man. We have examined the legacies of great men and have learned valuable lessons about becoming a godly man through the examples of the men who have gone before us.

- Manasseh demonstrated that it is never too late to start a new legacy of godliness.
- Jonathan reminded us that it is possible to break free of our father's ways and become a different man, devoted completely to God.
- Joshua showed us the need to be strong and courageous men who follow God, no matter where he leads.
- Phinehas taught us how to destroy the sins in our life.
- Caleb exemplified a heart of gratitude toward God that caused him to wholeheartedly serve him.
- We learned from Ananias how to submit our will to God's will.

- Joseph taught us the importance of living a sexually pure life before God.
- David showed us how to reject manpain and instead turn toward God's loving arms.
- Onesiphorus demonstrated how to be a loyal man.
- Aquila taught us how to support our wives.
- Boaz showed us how to treat God's precious daughters.
- Mark taught us to persevere instead of quitting.
- Mordecai showed us how to accept responsibility.
- Elijah and Bob (okay, Elisha) showed us how to have a healthy mentor/mentoree relationship.

It has been quite a ride together. However, it's not quite over yet. I want to end our journey together by looking at our "So What" chapter.

The title of this chapter presents us with an interesting question: What does it really matter if I become a godly man?

Why is it so important? Will it really make a difference in my life?

The answer to this question is a definitive "YES!" It will not only make a difference in our own lives, but it could greatly affect the lives of other men. That's the point I want to stress to you in this chapter.

While becoming a godly man should be the goal of every man, this chapter's topic goes beyond ourselves and reaches out to others. We are going to see how God can take all the hurt and pain of our past and use it to help other men.

The purpose of the first fourteen chapters of this book is to teach us what it is to be a godly man and give us the help needed to achieve this goal. The goal of this chapter is to show you that our journey is not a waste of time. It's worth the effort. Let me show you my point.

One night, I was sitting in front of the TV, watching a popular show. It had been a long, stressful day and I just wanted to sit down and let my brain wind down. However, this was not going to happen. My mind began working overtime as I was drawn into the show's story line.

One of the characters, a young man in his early twenties, was just days away from the birth of his first child. His wife was on bed rest, so he took her job at a local diner. While there, he was constantly asking questions and seeking advice from the owner of the diner, a man who really didn't want this young man bothering him.

As the show progressed, the young man revealed that when he was ten years old, his father had left him. Since his father had left no forwarding address, he figured he didn't want to be found.

Now, facing the birth of twin sons, he found himself terrified at the thought of being a father. He had nowhere to turn for advice and support, and he wanted to be a better father to his kids than his dad had been to him.

As I watched, I felt my heart break into a thousand pieces. I knew the pain that this young man felt. I, too, have a father who left me fearful and unprepared for life as a man. I remembered the pain of my father telling me I could never succeed as a minister and would never make a dime. I remembered the sense of fear and hopelessness as I licked my wounds from the latest round of verbal and emotional beatings from him. I recognized the feelings of hopelessness and pain that this young man felt, wondering if I was doomed to repeat my father's same mistakes.

Like the young man, I had reached out many times to other men in hope of support, advice, encouragement, and love. Like him, I had been denied help by men who just didn't want to be bothered. A few men tried to give me help along the way, but because of the distance between us, they couldn't give me the help I needed. My desire for a man to help me through these tough issues was for the most part ignored. I had no man to reach out and help me and tell me everything would be okay. Thankfully, God did provide me with a godly mother to help me through this time. I am extremely grateful to God for giving her to me and the influence she has had on my life. However, there were some times when it would have been less uncomfortable talking about certain things with a man.

As the show reached its conclusion, I wanted to just sit there and cry for the young man. I know it was only a TV show, but I longed to reach out, take him in my arms, and comfort him. Then I wanted to help him work through the grief and pain he was facing and let him know he wasn't doomed to repeat his dad's failure. I wanted to let him know everything would be all right and I would help him through his worries and fears. I never want another man to have to face the hurts and pain of both a father's rejection and the rejection of other Christian men who turned away from him in his hour of need.

It was at this moment I felt God speak to my heart. He said, **"This is only a tenth of the hurt and pain I feel every moment as I look at the faces of my men who feel alone and abandoned by their fathers. I long to be their Father, and I long for my children to rise up and be a support for these men."**

That's when it hit me. This was my calling in life. Everything that I have gone through has not been a waste. None of the pain, the heartache, not even a single tear was wasted. God can use all of the hurt and pain to help another young man who is dying inside from the emotional pain of his childhood.

I am the child of a loving heavenly Father. As his son, it is my duty to share this same love with other men who are longing for a father's love.

This book is a way of doing this. There are so many men who have gone through the things that I have faced in my life. Like me, they long for a man to reach out and love them. They want someone who can teach them how to get rid of all the garbage in their lives and help them become the strong, godly men they have the potential to be. Granted, they could work it out on their own, but why should they have to when

I have already gone through it and am working through to the other side?

As men, we need to step up to the plate and help the hurting young men all around us. We must help them reach their full potential as godly men. We need to come alongside of them and let them know that we love them.

They have to know we are committed to helping them as they go on their own journey to becoming a new man. We have faced it ourselves, we have learned how to change, and we have been working toward becoming a godly man.

> **WE MUST HELP OTHER MEN REACH THEIR POTENTIAL AS GODLY MEN!**

Now it is time to step up to the plate and reach out to help the other men who are hurting and dealing with the same things we have dealt with throughout our lives.

There are many examples of godly men in the Bible who have reached out and helped other hurting men.

Jesus reached out to the twelve disciples.

Jonathan mentored David. David in turn helped hundreds of hurting men. These same men later became known as the "Mighty Men."

Elijah helped Elisha reach his full potential as a godly man.

Eli mentored Samuel.

Moses trained Joshua.

The Bible is packed with man after man who worked through the hurt of his past and then reached out to other hurting men. Perhaps one of the best known examples of such a man is Paul. Let's take a moment and look at the way Paul reached out to a young man named Timothy and helped him become a godly man.

In Acts 16 we read that during Paul's second missionary journey, he and Silas visited the town of Lystra. While there, they met a young man named Timothy.

Paul came to Derbe and then to Lystra, where a disciple named Timothy lived, whose mother was Jewish and a believer but whose father was a Greek. The believers at Lystra and Iconium spoke well of him.

We can learn a great deal about Timothy in these verses, much of which may sound very familiar to many men today. He was raised by a believing mother and an unsaved father. His father was apparently absent from the home. He had either died or had deserted his family. Either way, Timothy was a young man in need of a strong male influence in his life. He had no example of a godly man in his home from which to draw strength and encouragement.

Timothy was a man who was deeply committed to becoming a godly man. He had a good reputation with the other people in the church. In 2 Timothy we read more about Timothy's walk with God.

I am reminded of your sincere faith, which first lived in your grandmother Lois and in your mother Eunice and, I am persuaded, now lives in you also (2 Timothy 1:5).

Timothy was raised under the godly influence of both his mother and grandmother. Paul knew the godly heart these two women possessed and that Timothy was blessed to receive the same type of heart. He also knew Timothy had a call on his life to do a great work for God.

Timothy, my son, I am giving you this command in keeping with the prophecies once made about you (1 Timothy 1:18).

Apparently, Timothy had been prophesied over before Paul came to town. The prophet revealed God's call on young Timothy's life. Paul heard all about the prophecy.

He knew all about Timothy's home life. He was aware that Timothy was a man in need of a strong, godly male influence in his life, so he did what any godly man would do. He took Timothy under his wing and became a father to him.

Paul took Timothy along with him on the rest of the missionary trips. He gave Timothy the one thing that was missing in his life, a strong, godly male role model. He showed Timothy how a godly man lives, acts, thinks, works, and ministers. He surrounded Timothy with other godly men like Luke and Silas. He literally adopted Timothy as his own son. Almost every time we see Paul address Timothy in the Bible, he calls him "my son." Paul helped Timothy achieve his potential as a godly man.

This is the mark of a true godly man. He deals with all of his past and then uses what he learned to help another man.

Paul definitely had a shady past to work through. Remember, he had formerly been Saul, the terrorist. He worked through all of that and become one of the godliest men to ever walk the face of the

> **THE YOUNG MEN NEED SOMEONE TO SHOW THEM HOW TO WORK THROUGH THE HURTS AND EMOTIONAL PAIN FROM THEIR PAST.**

earth. Now he took all he had learned about God and life and instilled it into another young man who desperately needed a male role model. He used the pain of his past to offer hope to another hurting man. We need to do the same.

Let's face it. Our world is full of young men who either have no father or who have fathers who are bad role models of a man. We are surrounded by abused men who are wounded and bleeding from the pain in their hearts.

These men are full of potential. They can all be used mightily by God. All they need is someone to show them how to work through the hurts and emotional pain from their past. They need instruction on how to break free of the things that hold them bound. They need someone to help them stop going down the destructive path they are on and to point them toward God and God's loving arms. They need someone to be the man and give them the love, acceptance, and guidance that was missing from their lives.

What about you?

Is there a young man you could be helping? Church youth groups are full of young men who are products of divorce or abandonment. Our children's departments are full of boys who are being raised by single moms who are doing the best job they can, yet can't be the male influence these boys need.

Can you reach out to them and become a godly influence in their lives? Could you be the man they seek out when they have questions or fears about their future? Could you be a source of encouragement to them in their time of need?

Ask God to give you his heart for the hurting men around you. Ask him to open doors for you to show his love to another young man. Ask him to show you that the pain you have experienced has not been in vain and that it can be used to show his love to another hurting man. When he places someone in your path, ask him for the right words and actions to help that young man. Then be obedient to what the Holy Spirit leads you to do.

You never know what changes you can make to a world full of hurting young men. Who knows what they will accomplish as they go through their own pursuit of becoming godly men, men with a heart to become more like Jesus. This is God's passion, it has become my passion, and I hope it will become your passion also.

As I bring this chapter to an end, I want to do something different. So far I have ended each chapter with a prayer for you to pray. However, as I bring this book to an end, I want to end this chapter with a prayer from me for you.

Dear heavenly Father, I thank you for all the years of extensive labor you have put into me so that I in turn could have the privilege of writing this book to help other men just like me. Father, please help the men who have read this book. They obviously have a desire to become godly men. I know that each of them has the potential to do this. Help them as they continue their journey.

Keep them safe and free from the enemy that seeks to destroy them and their mission to become like Jesus. Help them to work through all the hurt and pain in their past. Then send other men into their lives so that they can in turn help them. Keep them safe and watch over them.

I look forward to one day rejoicing with them in heaven as brothers and friends, united by a single cause: To become true, godly men whose whole life is centered around doing your will. In Jesus' name, amen

LEGACY CHALLENGES

1. Volunteer to work in your church youth group. I have never met a youth pastor who would refuse free help.

2. Begin a small group for young men. Pour yourself into the men that God leads to your group.

EXTREME LEGACY CHALLENGES

Volunteer to be a big brother or a mentor to another young man. Invest yourself in his life.

GROUP STUDY QUESTIONS

1. Have you had a man in your life whom you could turn to for help during your difficult times? How did it help you?

2. Can you relate to the Timothy's life?

3. Are you willing to make yourself vulnerable to another man so that you can help him deal with his hurts and pains and become a real man?

4. Are you willing to become a spiritual mentor/father to another young man?

5. How can your small group work together to help other men just beginning the journey to become real men, godly men?

SMALL GROUP
WORKBOOK

INTRODUCTION

All men want one thing in life...to be_____.

If you died today, what would be written on your tombstone?

What would you like to be written on your tombstone?

As long as we are still alive and breathing, we can continue to
_____our legacy. We can work to leave a legacy that
_____ _____ and encourages those we
leave behind.

We can live a life that _____!

CONTRACT BETWEEN YOU AND GOD

(AND YOUR MEN'S GROUP IF WORKING TOGETHER AS A GROUP)

Will you commit to:

Reading each chapter, including Scripture verses? Yes/No

Praying the prayers at the end of the chapter? Yes/No

Completing the homework assignments? Yes/No

Sincerely examine your heart using the questions at the end of each chapter? Yes/No

I, _____, am committed to
developing a godly legacy, a legacy that lasts.
I affirm this decision with my signature.

_____

(Sign)   (Date)

1 ✝ THE MANASSEH LEGACY

REALIZING THE NEED
TO START OVER

Manasseh shows every one of us that, no matter where we

_____ _____ or how big of a mess we

have made of our lives, it is _____ _____

_____ to start over and develop a new legacy of

godliness!

No man is too _____ _____ to start over and create

a new legacy! There is hope!

How did Manasseh start a new legacy?

    1.

    2.

    3.

What can you do to take these same actions in your life?

    1.

    2.

    3.

Read Deuteronomy 5:9. Write down what this verse speaks to you.

LEGACY THOUGHT TO REMEMBER

It is never too late to start a new, godly legacy!

LEGACY CHALLENGES

Spend time alone with God, and allow the Holy Spirit to show you how you would be remembered if you died today. This may be hard to see the truth about yourself, but realizing which areas need to change is step one to starting a new legacy.

EXTREME LEGACY CHALLENGES

This chapter discusses the steps Manasseh took to literally destroy his old legacy. Identify some steps you can take to destroy your sinful legacy.

- What changes need to be made?
- What must you stop doing?
- What must you start doing?

Ask these questions of a spouse or close, trusted friend or mentor and get his or her advice. Then start the process of beginning a new legacy.

GROUP STUDY QUESTIONS

1. Manasseh had developed a horrible legacy, yet was able to change. What areas of your life do you need to repent of and change to begin starting a new legacy?

2. We discussed Manasseh's breaking point where he realized he needed to humble himself. What was your breaking point?

3. Why is it important to take actions to dismantle our old legacy in order to start a new one? What does this involve for you?

4. What did the warning toward the end of the chapter mean to you?

5. Did you ever stop and think about the fact that the way you live your Christian life in front of your children could affect their eternal souls?

6. How would you feel if you knew your children went to hell because of the poor example you set before them of Christianity?

7. What can you do to ensure this doesn't happen?

8. If you are single, what changes do you need to make to your spiritual life before God blesses you with a wife and kids?

9. Read Deuteronomy 5:9–10. What does this passage say to you as you start the journey toward a Reborn Legacy?

2 ‡ THE JONATHAN LEGACY

THE SECOND VERSE
NOT THE SAME AS THE FIRST

No man is ever doomed to repeat his _____'s
mistakes.

List the three areas Jonathan differed from his father:

1.

2.

3.

What does each of these points speak to you personally?

1.

2.

3.

How can you improve yourself in each of these areas?

1.

2.

3.

LEGACY THOUGHT TO REMEMBER:

You can break free of any generational patterns in your life! There is no area of your life that can't develop the heart of a godly man and succeed. It will take hard work and a willingness to make changes, but in the end it will be worth it.

LEGACY CHALLENGES

Make a list of all the areas in which you do not want to follow your father. Then develop a battle plan to make changes to become different.

EXTREME LEGACY CHALLENGES

If possible, discuss with your dad or other family members why your father did what he did or is the way he is. Don't be judgmental or hard on him. Be gentle and approach it from the point that you just want to understand why. This information can help you forgive your dad. This will allow you to be free to pursue a new life course.

GROUP STUDY QUESTIONS

1. What is your relationship with your father like?

2. Was there a point when you found out that your father wasn't what you thought he was? Do you want to turn out like your dad?

3. What actions must stop and what changes must happen so that you don't end up like your dad?

4. Did your father have a relationship with God? How did this affect your view of God?

5. Was your father a family man? Did he put his family's needs first?

6. What was your father's work ethic like? How did he view his job? How did this affect your view of work?

7. In the extreme homework, forgiving your father is discussed. Why is this important?

8. How can we as a group work together to start new legacies of godliness?

3 ‡ THE JOSHUA LEGACY

STANDING STRONG
AND COURAGEOUS

In life, _____ keeps you from moving forward
while _____ brings you victory.

Every man has a call on his life. God has called us all to be

_____ and _____!

List some ways the enemy is attacking men today:

1.

2.

3.

4.

What can you do to help defeat these attacks?

What are some cliffs God is calling you to courageously leap off in your life?

List steps you can take to courageously walk to the cliff and find strength to leap into God's calling on your life:

LEGACY THOUGHT TO REMEMBER:

A man can never realize his full potential in God's kingdom until he comes to the place where he is willing to conquer his fears and be strong and courageous. Our world is crying out for men who will be strong and courageous! You can be that kind of man!

LEGACY CHALLENGES

God told Joshua that part of being strong and courageous was following the commands found in the Word of God, no matter what the cost. The only way to know God's Word is to read God's Word, so commit to a daily Bible reading plan. Places like Biblegateway.com have Bible reading plans they will send you daily via e-mail. Utilize such a plan so you can begin hiding God's Word in your heart.

EXTREME LEGACY CHALLENGES

Ask yourself, "What is one thing I can do for God's kingdom that I am too scared to do in my own strength?"

Then find a way to do it. Examples may be starting a ministry at your church, witnessing more, stepping into a leadership position at church, etc.

GROUP STUDY QUESTIONS

1. What is your cliff, the thing God is asking you to courageously step up and do for him?

2. Has fear kept you from doing something God has asked you to do? Why?

3. What would be accomplished for the kingdom of God if you overcame this fear?

4. How can being strong and courageous make a difference in your family?

5. How can being strong and courageous make a difference in your church?

6. How can being strong and courageous make a difference in your community?

7. How can we as a group work together to become strong and courageous men?

4 ‡ THE PHINEHAS LEGACY
BEING A MAN OF ZEAL

A man of zeal has a _____ to destroy
_____ before it destroys him!

Phinehas loved God so much that he was_____
for God's sake. He hated that this man was in essence
_____on God. He felt the same pain that God
was feeling and he took action to put an end to it.

A godly man has a zeal for _____.
Whatever it takes, he will destroy sin in his life. It is time
we follow the words found in the book of John and become
_____ as God is _____.

What are some areas that you need to change to remove sin in your
life?

In what areas do you see compromise creeping into your life?

What steps can you take to destroy this sin and compromise?

LEGACY THOUGHT TO REMEMBER:

A zealous man will see his sin as an offense against the holiness of God. Like Phinehas, he will bring the boom and drive a spear through it with all the vigor he possesses because he wants to become as godly a man as possible.

LEGACY CHALLENGES

Ask the Holy Spirit to show you areas of sin that stand between you and God. Make a list and repent of the sins. Stop doing the sin and change your behavior.

EXTREME LEGACY CHALLENGES

In this chapter, I mentioned that God required me to mail a check and ask forgiveness from my college in order to break the habit of lying. Is there sin in your life that you need to make restitution for? Do it. Ask the Holy Spirit how you could make it right. It may be embarrassing, but it is the fastest way to destroy the sin in your life.

GROUP STUDY QUESTIONS

1. Do you understand why we need a zeal for God?

2. Do you believe you have a freedom in Christ to sin, or do you believe you need to pursue holiness?

3. Are there areas of sin in your life that you tolerate?

4. How can you go about removing these sins from your life?

5. How can we as a group help you kill the areas of sin in your life?

6. How can we as a group work together to ensure compromise doesn't creep into our men's group? Our families? Our church?

5 ‡ THE CALEB LEGACY

STARTING STRONG, FINISHING WELL

Caleb was _____ to God for his freedom.

God was his new Master and he would never _____

_____ to his old life again!

Caleb was not going to quit on God no matter what the rest of the nation said or did. He was moving forward _____ or _____ the rest of the people!

What was the difference between the Caleb and Joshua and the other ten spies?

What needs to change inside of you so you are more like Caleb and less like the other spies?

Caleb was wholeheartedly devoted to God until the day of his death. What steps do you need to take in your life so you not only start strong, but finish well?

LEGACY THOUGHT TO REMEMBER:

This is the mark of a godly man: No matter what happens in life, he is grateful to God and follows him wholeheartedly. This is a man God can use. We need to start strong, and finish well as we wholeheartedly serve God.

LEGACY CHALLENGES

Ask God to reveal to you areas that you are not wholeheartedly following him. Make a list of any areas that are not completely surrendered to God. Then repent of them and make any necessary changes.

EXTREME LEGACY CHALLENGES

Ask your mentor and/or a trusted friend or family member if they see an area in your life where you are not wholeheartedly devoted to God or have a tendency to go back to your old life. Don't be defensive when they honestly answer you.

GROUP STUDY QUESTIONS

1. What does it mean to be wholeheartedly devoted to God?

2. Are you wholeheartedly devoted to God?

3. What are you grateful to God for freeing you from? How can you express this gratitude?

4. Is there anything holding you back from serving God wholeheartedly?

5. We mentioned Caleb defeated all of his enemies. What are some of the enemies you must defeat? How are you going to defeat them?

6. Can the words God spoke describing Caleb be used to describe you?

6 ‡ THE ANANIAS LEGACY
THE NO HIGHWAY OPTION

_____ to God and his will is the
true mark of a godly man.

When a soldier receives his orders, he isn't given an option if he
wants to do it or not—he does it! We are _____in
God's army and God is our _____

_____.

As you submit your will to God's you will learn his will is
_____ for you, and you will want to submit more.

In what area do you struggle submitting to God in your life?

What changes can you make or what steps can you take to overcome this struggle?

LEGACY THOUGHT TO REMEMBER:

We need to decide whether we are going to submit to God's will or not. It is as basic as that. It involves one step: When God gives the orders, OBEY!

LEGACY CHALLENGES

Every morning begin your day by telling God you want to surrender your will to his will today. Ask him to make clear to you what his will is for you. Then do it.

Make a list of all the times you can remember not submitting to God's will for you and ask him to forgive you. Be specific.

EXTREME LEGACY CHALLENGES

Is there someone that you have felt led to witness to but for one reason or another been afraid to do so? Submit your will to God and witness to the person—who knows what the end result could be. The person may reject it, or may get saved and go on and lead thousands to Christ. Take the chance and submit to God and leave it in his hands.

GROUP STUDY QUESTIONS

1. Do you feel that it is correct to say Ananias was scared to step out and do what God was telling him to do?

2. Do you agree with the statement that God is our commanding officer and to not follow orders is sin? Why?

3. Do you believe God already knew Ananias would submit before he asked him?

4. How does this statement "submission to God is the way we express love to him" make you feel?

5. Do you agree that Ananias will share in the rewards of Saul's years in ministry?

6. Are there things you feel that God wants you to do that you haven't submitted to him by obeying?

7. Are there things that God doesn't want you to do that you don't want to stop doing?

8. Will you choose to submit to the areas in questions 7 and 8?

7 ⳾ THE DAVID LEGACY
CONQUERING MANPAIN

_____ is the deep, emotional pain and wounds inside of us. These wounds are the pain of unmet needs every man has for a _____'s _____ and approval.

We can only _____ our pain for so long. It will eventually come out. Left undealt with, we will begin to _____ just like the man who caused our manpain.

How has manpain affected your life?

What was the source of your manpain?

How can does prayer and developing a relationship with God help us overcome manpain?

LEGACY THOUGHT TO REMEMBER:

Only God can remove your manpain. He can take your broken, wounded, and battered heart and fill it with love. Then you will be free to become a man after God's own heart. All he requires is that you face the pain, bring it to him, and allow him to love and heal you.

LEGACY CHALLENGES

In order to deal with your manpain, you need to first face that it is there. Spend time with God in prayer asking him to show you:
1. Who caused your manpain?
2. How manpain affects your daily life.
3. How manpain affects your relationships.
4. How manpain affects your spiritual life.
5. What you do to ease your manpain.

Then ask God to heal your manpain. Ask God to fill the needs in your life. Ask him to be the one that meets the needs for love and acceptance so you can break free of manpain and live as a victorious son of God.

EXTREME LEGACY CHALLENGES

In this chapter, I discussed how I had to come to the place of showing mercy to my father and realize he too suffered from manpain. Honestly look at the life and background of the people who caused your manpain. What in their past caused them to act the way they did? You need to do this, not to excuse their behavior, but to help you overcome. You need to have mercy on them and look at them through the eyes of an adult, not the eyes of a hurting child in need of love and acceptance. After you do this, share what you discovered with a trusted friend or mentor.

GROUP STUDY QUESTIONS

1. How has manpain affected your life?

2. Who caused your manpain?

3. We mentioned some men turn to sex, drugs, alcohol, success, etc., to fill their manpain. What do you turn to ease your manpain?

4. Did you have a Jonathan in your life? Was he able to fill your needs?

5. We said David reached his breaking point with Nabal and he snapped, ready to give Nabal his years of pent-up manpain. Have you experienced a breaking point? What was it? How did you react?

6. We discussed how David was vulnerable with God and expressed all his thoughts with God, both the good and the bad. Do you do this with God? If the answer is no, why not?

7. How does prayer help us overcome manpain?

8. How can we as a group help you face your manpain?

8 ‡ THE JOSEPH LEGACY

STAYING PURE IN
AN IMPURE WORLD

We have a responsibility before _____ to stay sexually pure. While sexual sin affects a lot of people, it is really a _____ against _____.

To have pre-marital sex or an affair is to be anti-_____ and anti-_____.

We are more _____ for an attack after we have successfully _____ the previous attack.

What are the three ways listed in this chapter to overcome sexual temptation?

1.

2.

3.

How is sinning sexually sinning against God?

We discussed the need to develop both a battle plan and an escape plan when dealing with sexual temptation. Write your plan here:

LEGACY THOUGHT TO REMEMBER:

Whenever the New Testament discusses the subject of sexual temptation, it gives one command: RUN! The Bible does not tell us to reason with it. It tells us to FLEE! We cannot yield to sensuality if we are running away from it. Run for your life. Get out of there! If we try to reason with lust or entertain sexual thoughts, we will give in to them. We won't be able to fight it. This is why God forcefully orders us to run away from it.

LEGACY CHALLENGES

1. Identify the areas of your life that cause you to be tempted to sin sexually. Write down a clear battleplan to overcome.
2. Take a sheet of paper and, through the power of the Holy Spirit, identify times you have sinned sexually. Include any TV shows, movies, magazines, thoughts, and actions. Then spend time in prayer confessing these sins to God. Ask him to forgive you. Ask God to restore your mind to purity and holiness like his. Begin to live a pure and holy life before God.

3. In the future, keep a short account with God. Anytime a thought to sin sexually enters your mind, cast it down in Jesus' name. Confess it and move on, continuing the pursuit of sexual purity.

EXTREME LEGACY CHALLENGES

1. For one month do not watch any TV or any movies. Instead take that time and spend it reading the Bible. You will be surprised at the end of the month how little your conscience will allow you to watch after renewing your mind.

2. Begin using the V-chip on your TV and install a Internet filtering program on your computer. Have someone else set the override passwords.

3. Read *Every Man's Battle* and *Tactics* By Fred Stoeker.

GROUP STUDY QUESTIONS

1. When was the first time you were exposed to pornography or sexual temptation? What do you remember thinking or feeling in that moment?

2. How is society's view of a real man and God's view of sexual purity different?

3. What part of this chapter stood out to you the most? What area needs the most work?

4. What are your thoughts on the idea that both Satan and God are trying to kill you?

5. How do you feel about Jesus' statement that looking at a woman lustfully is the same as having sex with her?

6. How does the idea that a real man runs away from spiritual temptation instead of staying and reasoning sound to you?

7. How can a V-chip for your TV help you?

8. Do you think the idea of not being alone with a woman is a good idea or not? Why?

9. What may taking a stand cost you? What will not taking a stand cost you?

10. What is your final decision, to be like Joseph or like the man in Proverbs 7?

9 ‡ THE BOAZ LEGACY
BECOMING A LADIES' MAN

A true ladies man is a man who treats all woman as what they really are—_____'s

_____ _____!

What are the four lessons we learned from Boaz about how to treat women:

1.

2.

3.

4.

Which of these steps is the hardest for you? Why?

What are steps you can take to grow in each of these areas?

Lesson 1:

Lesson 2:

Lesson 3:

Lesson 4:

LEGACY THOUGHT TO REMEMBER:

A real ladies' man in a man who treats women with dignity and respect. He treats them as what they really are, daughters of the Almighty God!

LEGACY CHALLENGES

Sit down with a piece of paper and write down all the ways you can think of that society defines a ladies' man. Then make another list of what the Bible says about the first list you made. Then repent of times you followed society's view.

EXTREME LEGACY CHALLENGES

Take the second list you just made of how the Bible contradicts the world's view of a ladies' man. Then use a concordance or an online search to find a verse in the Bible that directly contradicts the world's lies of how to view women. Memorize the verse.

GROUP STUDY QUESTIONS

1. This chapter discussed how Boaz interacted with and treated Ruth. What does the fact that Ruth was not an Israelite tell us about how God's men should treat unsaved women?

2. Of the four points discussed in this chapter, which are you strongest in doing?

3. Of the four points discussed in this chapter, in which area do you struggle the most?

4. How can deceit affect relationships?

5. We mentioned that men need to put the desires of women ahead of our own. Why is this so hard for men to do?

6. How do we overcome and do it?

7. How can we as a group help each other apply the lesson from Boaz's legacy to our lives?

10 ✦ THE MORDECAI LEGACY

BECOMING A RESPONSIBLE MAN

We need to strive to be responsible, dependable men in

_____ _____of our lives.

We need to take responsibility for the family God has given to us. A godly man doesn't _____ or

_____…he _____!

God never gets tired of _____ us.
He wants us to be dependable men who can be _____
with more and more.

What is the biggest area in which you struggle with being responsible?

Why is this area such a struggle for you?

What are some steps you can take to overcome your struggle and grow in your level of responsibility?

1.

2.

3.

LEGACY THOUGHT TO REMEMBER:

Responsibility is only developed one way: through lots of hard work. You must face the truth about yourself and then begin to do the things you have previously shied away from doing. It can only be done through hard work, perseverance, a desire to change, and most importantly, the power of God.

LEGACY CHALLENGES

1. Make a list of all the areas in your life that you have failed at being responsible. Then repent to God and the people your actions affected. Make a plan on how you can grow in this area.

2. Look for ways to lighten the load on those around you. Step up and help them with their responsibilities.

3. Learn to be financially responsible. If you don't have a budget, make one! Work as a family and develop a budget that everyone can participate in. If you are single, make a budget for yourself and stick to it.

EXTREME LEGACY CHALLENGES

I have found that the people around me can see areas where I am lacking responsibility more clearly than I can. While it is hard to hear, I have found their assessment of me to be very beneficial in areas where I need to grow. Ask the people in your life if they see any areas in which you are irresponsible. Be open to their feedback and make changes.

GROUP STUDY QUESTIONS

1. What is responsibility?

2. Are there areas in your life that need to be stretched so you can be more responsible?

3. How does responsibility relate to your job?

4. How does responsibility relate to your emotions?

5. How does responsibility relate to your finances?

6. How does responsibility relate to your relationships with God and others?

11 ‡ THE ELIJAH LEGACY

MENTORING THE
NEXT GENERATION

We have a generation of _____s who need an

_____ to mentor them!

If you multiply two times zero, you get zero. We cannot continue be-

ing _____ in God's kingdom. We need to give

younger men something to _____

off of.

Who was an Elijah in your life?

List things in his life you admire and want to see a double portion in

your life:

What are some ways you can be an Elijah to another younger man?

LEGACY THOUGHT TO REMEMBER:

"My generation's ceiling is the next generation's floor." We should encourage the next generation to surpass us spiritually! We should never discourage them in order to promote ourselves and our interests. A real man of God hopes the next generation goes above and beyond what he is doing and then do all he can to help them do it!

LEGACY CHALLENGES

1. Daily pray that God leads you to an Elijah to mentor and disciple you. Also ask God to help you to become a mentor to an Elisha.
2. Honestly ask yourself, "What would be my response if a man I am mentoring surpassed me spiritually?" Take this answer to God and ask him to help you to encourage them to go further than you can go.

EXTREME LEGACY CHALLENGES

Find an activity at your church, like being a youth worker or a Royal Rangers leader, and start investing in the lives of the younger men in your church, especially the ones who don't have a dad in their lives. Go beyond just working at church and make it a part of your everyday life, being a spiritual father to all boys/teens.

GROUP STUDY QUESTIONS

1. Why did Elisha not want to leave Elijah? What was the cause of his devotion?

2. What do you make of Elijah's response to Elisha's request?

3. Are you more like Elijah, Elisha, or are you like both?

4. Is there an Elijah in your life you can model yourself after? How do you plan to do it?

5. Two times zero is still zero. What are some steps to take to make sure we aren't zeroes?

6. Are you secure enough to be Elijah and help the next generation grow?

12 ‡ THE AQUILA LEGACY

LEARNING TO SUPPORT YOUR WIFE

When opposition and turbulent times come, a godly man takes steps to ensure that the strength of his marriage stays the same by _____ with his wife.

A godly man will _____ his wife to become all she can be, and will _____ all that he can to help her reach her goal.

Write down the three areas this chapter discussed that a man of God needs to support his wife:

1.

2.

3.

What area do you need to grown in?

What steps can you take to grow in this area?

LEGACY THOUGHT TO REMEMBER:

A godly man will encourage his wife to become all that she can be, and will do all that he can to help her reach that goal. He should admire her and seek ways to increase himself to grow alongside of her. He should try and help her fulfill her dreams. He should praise her and build her up. Her success should be his greatest joy.

LEGACY CHALLENGES

1. Ask your wife if she feels secure about life with you. Honestly listen and make any necessary changes.

2. Sit down with your wife and discuss with her any dreams or visions she has that she wants to fulfill. Then think of ways you can encourage her or help her accomplish her dreams.

3. Read the book *Every Man's Marriage* by Fred Stoeker.

EXTREME LEGACY CHALLENGES

Volunteer to do some form of service together at your church. Some ideas: Lead a Sunday school class, prepare a meal for an event at church, clean the church together, etc. Be creative, but make sure you serve together as a team.

GROUP STUDY QUESTIONS

1. We discussed the need your wife has for security and how it is your job to ensure her security. Discuss this and different ways it can be accomplished.

2. How well do you work with your wife? What are some steps you can take to work better together?

3. How do you react in times of crisis? Is this beneficial or harmful to your wife's sense of security?

4. Do you and your wife ever minister together? What are some ways you can do this?

5. Do you encourage your wife to become all that she can be, and do you do all that you can to help her reach her goals?

6. How often do you praise and build up your wife?

7. Is your wife's success a source of joy to you or does it make you feel inferior? Why?

8. How does the way that Jesus treated the church relate to how you should treat your wife?

13 ‡ THE ONESIPHORUS LEGACY

BEING A LOYAL MAN

Men cannot continue to support a _____
of men they have never met, but not support their fellow
_____ in need.

A man who wants to become like Jesus will _____
and help a _____ no matter what he is
facing.

What causes you to have a lack of loyalty?

How can you work to strengthen loyalty in your life?

LEGACY THOUGHT TO REMEMBER:

The world needs a Christian community where the men can stand side by side, holding each other up through whatever they face. They need to see men who are loyal to their wives and never even consider the idea of divorce. They desire to see men who are loyal to their children and stay. They need men who are able to reach the unsaved, and have the new believer know that Christian men can be trusted to stand by them and not cut and run.

LEGACY CHALLENGES:

Take time alone and examine your relationships. Dissect whether or not you are truly loyal to the people in your life. Do the same with your past relationships. Repent if necessary and take action to change.

EXTREME LEGACY CHALLENGES

Find someone who is going through a rough time. For example, find a man who is undergoing a serious family illness or injury, or find a man who is struggling to deal with pain from his past. If you can't think of anyone, ask your pastor. Then go to this person and give him all the help possible. Stay committed to him and see him through his crisis.

GROUP STUDY QUESTIONS

1. What do you consider a loyal man to be? Do you think you are this way?

2. Have you ever had people desert you in a time of need? Have you ever done this to others?

3. Would you be willing to help and comfort a friend if it endangered your personal safety and comfort?

4. How does loyalty relate to a marriage? If asked, do you think your wife would say you are loyal?

5. We read that Onesiphorus traveled from Ephesus to Rome to see Paul, a trip over hundreds of miles. Would you do the same for a friend in need?

6. What are some ways that you can improve in the area of loyalty?

14 ‡ THE MARK LEGACY
LEARNING TO QUIT QUITTING

We need to face the behavioral pattern of quitting, deal with it, and become a man who _____.

If we want to develop _____, we need to develop _____.

What are some areas in your life you have quit?

What caused you to quit?

What needs to change inside of you to develop perseverance?

What steps can you take to make these changes?

LEGACY THOUGHT TO REMEMBER:

A godly man believes God will do what he promised to do. He believes that God is true to his Word. He never stops believing no matter who else doubts, criticizes, mocks, or persecutes him. Quitting is never an option!

LEGACY CHALLENGES

Make a list of every time you have ever quit something or have run away from a situation. Analyze what caused this reaction inside of you. Then repent and ask God to forgive you. Determine to never quit again. Finally, examine the list you made and finish what you quit. This will help you develop perseverance.

EXTREME LEGACY CHALLENGES

Find one thing that you quit in your life and finish it. For example, maybe it's time to finish that project you started on your home and never quite wrapped up. Perhaps you need to take a few classes and finish your degree. Whatever it may be, finish something you quit and turn your failure into a personal victory.

GROUP STUDY QUESTIONS

1. As a child, did you quit a lot of things? Did it carry on into your adult life?

2. Have you ever taken the time to analyze why you quit things? What did you discover?

3. Have you ever quit on God?

4. We mentioned the devastating effects Mark's quitting had on Paul's ministry team. Has your quitting affected other people?

5. What is perseverance? How does is it relate to character development?

6. I made the statement that quitting can lead to backsliding. How does this happen?

7. What can you do to make up for all the times you have quit? What action can you take?

CONCLUSION

SO WHAT? WHAT DOES IT REALLY MATTER IF I DEVELOP A GODLY LEGACY?

We need to create a new legacy of godliness so God can take all the hurt and pain of our past and use it to help

_____   _____.

We must help other men reach their full

_____as _____ men!

What can you do to help another man experience the same freedom in Christ that you have experienced?

List three ways you could influence young men in your sphere of influence, young men that you can "spiritually adopt" and help grow in their walk with God:

1.

2.

3.

Will you commit to one of these ways? Yes/No

LEGACY THOUGHT TO REMEMBER:

Our world is full of young men who either have no father or who have fathers who are bad role models. We are surrounded by abused men who are wounded and bleeding from the pain in their hearts. These men are full of potential. They can all be used mightily by God. All they need is someone to show them how to work through the hurts and emotional pain from their past. They need instruction on how to break free of the things that hold them bound. They need someone to help them stop going down the destructive path they are on and to point them toward God and God's loving arms. They need someone to be the man and give them the love, acceptance, and guidance that was missing from their lives. YOU CAN BE THAT MAN!

LEGACY CHALLENGES

1. Volunteer to work in your church youth group. I have never met a youth pastor who would refuse free help.

2. Begin a small group for young men. Pour yourself into the men that God leads to your group.

EXTREME LEGACY CHALLENGES

Volunteer to be a big brother or a mentor to another young man. Invest yourself in his life.

GROUP STUDY QUESTIONS

1. Have you had a man in your life whom you could turn to for help during your difficult times? How did it help you?

2. Can you relate to the Timothy's life?

3. Are you willing to make yourself vulnerable to another man so that you can help him deal with his hurts and pains and become a real man?

4. Are you willing to become a spiritual mentor/father to another young man?

5. How can your small group work together to help other men just beginning the journey to become real men, godly men?

WORKBOOK FILL-IN ANSWERS

INTRODUCTION

1. remembered 2. write, honors God 3. lasts

CHAPTER 1

1. came from, never too late 2. far gone

CHAPTER 2

1. father's

CHAPTER 3.

1. fear, courage 2. strong, courageous

CHAPTER 4

1. passion, sin 2. jealous, cheating 3. holiness, holy, holy

CHAPTER 5

1. grateful, go back 2. with, without

CHAPTER 6

1. Submitting 2. soldiers, 5-star General 3. best

CHAPTER 7

1. Manpain, man's love 2. bury, act

CHAPTER 8

1. God, sin, God 2. God, family 3. vulnerable, resisted

CHAPTER 9

1. God's precious daughters

CHAPTER 10

1. all areas 2. leave, abandon, stays 3. stretching, trusted

CHAPTER 11

1. Elishas, Elijah 2. zeroes, multiply

CHAPTER 12

1. working 2. encourage, do

CHAPTER 13

1. team, brothers 2. support, friend

CHAPTER 14

1. perseveres 2. character, perseverance

CONCLUSION

1. other men 2. potential, godly

Jamie loves to speak to men and is available to speak at your next men's event. Jamie combines humor and his personal testimony to both engage and challenge men to grow in their walk with God. He uses his testimony of overcoming abuse as well as dealing with his physical and emotional issues growing up to encourage men that no matter what their background or where they have come from in life, they can grow into mighty men in God's kingdom.

"Years ago, while I was attending the University of Valley Forge, God gave me a deep desire to minister to men. My calling is to help men learn what it means to be a godly man and how to develop a deep, personal relationship with their heavenly Father. We strive to challenge and encourage men to reach their full potential in God's kingdom."

If you are interested in having Jamie at your next men's event as a speaker or workshop leader, or if you are interested in having him come share with your church, e-mail him at jamie@mantourministries.com. He is also available to speak for one or multiple weeks on the theme of his books, *Putting On Manhood* and *Legacy: Living a Life that Lasts*.

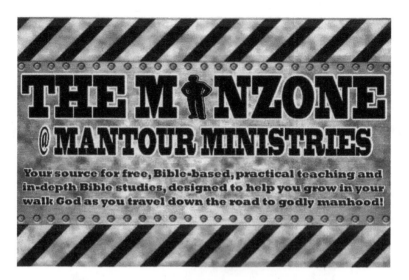

Visit The Manzone at Mantour Ministries for monthly articles, Bible studies, and videos, all designed for men.
www.mantourministries.com

ARE YOU INTERESTED IN BRINGING THE MANTOUR CONFERENCES TO YOUR AREA? WE WOULD LOVE TO SPEAK TO YOU ABOUT THE POSSIBILITY OF HOSTING A CONFERENCE! CONTACT US TODAY AT INFO@MANTOURMINISTRIES.COM!

ALSO FOR MEN

PUTTING ON MANHOOD

This book will show you how to put childish ways behind you and become the man God designed you to be. Each chapter provides questions for reflection, making it an excellent tool for individual or small group study.

Visit **mantourministries.com** for details.

Also available in both print and digital formats
from Amazon, BarnesandNoble.com,
and other online retailers.